CARNIVAL OF
FELTING

GILLIAN HARRIS

CARNIVAL OF FELTING

BEAUTIFUL ACCESSORIES FOR YOU AND YOUR HOME

St. Martin's Griffin
New York

www.stmartins.com

Library of Congress Cataloging-in-Publication Data
Available Upon Request

ISBN 978-1-250-02493-0

Originally published by Collins & Brown

First St. Martin's Griffin Edition: February 2013

10 9 8 7 6 5 4 3 2 1

CONTENTS

••••••••••••••••••••••••

INTRODUCTION

◆◆◆◆◆◆◆◆◆◆◆◆◆◆◆◆◆◆◆

Florals and vintage style have always played a tremendous part in my designs. I am hugely influenced by flowers and all of nature's wonders, but my main source of fascination and inspiration comes from color.

As feltmaking has increased in popularity over recent years, colorful wool tops have become more widely available, giving us all a more varied and interesting palette to work with. I often use the wool just like watercolor paint, using its translucency and fluidity to create washes of color and overlays, but equally I like to use bold blocks of solid color, and for me, having a great selection of colors to work with is vital, and often provides sufficient inspiration alone!

With that in mind, I wanted the projects in this book to evoke a feeling of carnival—an exciting and stimulating vision of color. Colors that sit happily together and colors you wouldn't have dreamt would be neighbors, dance merrily alongside one another when they are magically transformed into fluffy felt creations for you to make!

My latest collection of designs is intended both for those of you who have never made felt before, and the more experienced amongst you, looking perhaps for some new ideas and inspirations, or to add some different techniques to your basic feltmaking skills.

If you are a beginner or just looking for a memory refresh, the Techniques section at the back of the book has everything you need to know about equipment, materials and all the different felting techniques covered in the projects. But in addition to covering basic techniques, I have tried to add new and interesting perspectives to the felting processes, with which you can take this magical craft one step further, for example "precision" wet felting, that is making sure your piece of felt looks as you'd intended it to when it's finished!

Another aim is to share the way I use different feltmaking techniques together on one project. I think this creates more visual interest and provides the scope for more detail. Take Candy-Coated Cupcake Tea Cozy as an example, where I have used a precision wet felted base with raised details added afterward using felting needles, or the Bewitching Butterfly Curtain that combines nuno felting (onto fabric) and wet felting. The possibilities are endless!

Finally, and most importantly, whether you are using my designs as an inspiration, or following each project down to the very last detail, please make sure you enjoy yourself during the process! The wonderful art of feltmaking is incredibly forgiving. It lends itself brilliantly and uniquely to "the art of the imperfect". Let go of "immaculate squares" and "perfect edges", and just have fun creating and manipulating wool and seeing what is possible—maybe with a view to using your own designs and ideas in the future.

Gillian Harris

ACCESSORIES FOR YOU...YOU...YOU

FLORIBUNDA FOLLY EVENING BAG

◆◆◆◆◆◆◆◆◆◆◆◆◆◆◆◆◆◆◆◆◆◆◆◆◆

When it's time to put on your LBD (little black dress) and you're ready to party, this head-turning bag, adorned with a spectacular array of roses, is your ultimate accessory. The bag shape is wet felted using a plastic template and the roses are added afterward. Make the felt handles your desired length to finish it off nicely.

TECHNIQUES
3-D SEAMLESS OBJECTS
(PAGE 124),
NEEDLE FELTING
(PAGE 134),
MAKING A
HANDLE/STRAND
(PAGE 130)

MATERIALS

◆◆◆◆◆◆◆◆◆◆◆◆◆◆◆◆◆◆

MERINO WOOL TOPS

3 oz (75 g) of white for the inner layer
3 oz (75 g) of custard yellow for the middle layer
$2/3$ oz (20 g) each of cherry red, retro red, salmon pink, custard yellow, and gold for the outer layer
1 oz (25 g) of cherry red for handles (or longer if desired)

OTHER REQUIREMENTS

Wet felting essentials (see page 116)
Strong template plastic
Five felt roses and felt for leaves (see notes below)
Strong fabric glue
38-gauge felting needle and foam

Finished size: 11 x 9 in. (28 x 23 cm) excluding handles

NOTES

The roses are made following the instructions for the Rose and Daisy Corsages, page 22. I have made my flowers from combinations of the wool top colors used for the bag: two from gold/custard yellow; one from salmon pink/custard yellow/gold; one from retro red/salmon pink; and one from cherry red/retro red. The leaves are made and cut from a flat piece of pale yellow olive with a small amount of dark olive for the needle felted veins.

METHOD

❖❖❖❖❖❖❖❖❖❖❖❖❖❖❖❖❖❖❖❖❖❖❖❖❖❖❖❖

WET FELTING THE BAG SHAPE

1. Using the template on page 136, enlarge by 200%, or to at least 20% bigger than you intend your final bag to be to allow for shrinkage. Cut out the bag shape from strong template plastic.

2. Lay out a layer of white wool vertically, overlapping the edges of the template. Cover with netting, wet, soap and rub for a few minutes. Turn the template over and fold in the edges. Repeat on the other side to complete the inner layer.

3. For the middle layer, repeat step 2 using the custard yellow, but lay the wool in the opposite direction—horizontally— remembering to fold in the seam overlap each time you turn.

4. For the outer layer, the wool tops are laid out so they gradate in color. Start from the base with the cherry red and lay the wool vertically, allowing for a larger than normal overlap. Use the wool wispily and overlap the wispy ends as you lay them out. Work through from cherry red to retro red, then onto salmon pink to custard yellow, finishing up with the gold at the top.

5. Cover, wet, soap and rub for about 20–30 minutes, or until all the fibers are securely attached together. Turn over and fold in the edges.

6. Now working on the final side, continue to lay down the wool tops, gradating the colors as in step 4, but DO NOT overlap the edges this time. Cover, wet, soap and rub for 30 minutes or until all the fibers are well felted together.

7. Briefly rinse in warm water, then do a complete roll on both sides as described on page 127 (see 3-d Seamless Objects, step 9). Rinse under very hot water, then roll briefly again.

8. Using small sharp scissors, cut along the top of the bag and remove the template. Trim to neaten edges if necessary, and then wet, soap and rub for about five minutes until felted.

FORMING THE BAG BASE

1. Make the felt quite wet and very soapy, and place it on a table. Rubbing from the inside, start to form a base, using the soap to help shape and sculpt. Keep working it until it can stand up, checking that it looks even from all angles.

2. Rinse again in very hot then very cold water, making sure all traces of soap are removed. Roll again until you are happy with the shrinkage, then re-shape and leave to dry.

MAKING AND ATTACHING THE HANDLES

1. Referring to Making a Handle/Strand, page 130, make two handles from the cherry red wool tops.

2. Mark with pins where you want the handles to be and make a small hole for each with the sharp pointed ends of your scissors. Push each handle end through from the inside of the bag to the outside, and secure with a tight knot.

ADDING THE FLORAL TRIM

1. Attach the five felt roses to the bag front using matching thread and strong fabric glue.

2. Referring to Simple Flat Felt, page 120, make a small piece of flat felt from the pale yellow olive wool tops. Cut five leaves from it, and needle on the veins using dark olive. Sew in place.

TIP
You can change the position or
length of the handles according
to your personal preferences.

❖❖❖❖❖❖❖❖❖❖❖❖❖❖❖❖❖

A WOOLLY EMBRACE
COBWEBBY SCARF

✦✦✦✦✦✦✦✦✦✦✦✦✦✦✦✦✦✦✦✦✦✦✦

This short yet luxurious cowl-like scarf can be made as cobwebby as you like and it will still keep you as warm as toast when there's a chill in the air. The swirling flowery design is the same on both sides as the wool is laid out only one layer thick, and the small opening toward one end makes it easy to do up.

TECHNIQUES
SIMPLE FLAT FELT
(PAGE 120)

MATERIALS

✦✦✦✦✦✦✦✦✦✦✦✦✦✦✦✦

MERINO WOOL TOPS
1 oz (25 g) each of pale turquoise and dark olive
Smaller amounts of white,
candy pink, red, and bright yellow

OTHER REQUIREMENTS
Wet felting essentials (see notes below and on page 116)

Finished size: 33 x 12 in. (84 x 30 cm) at widest point

NOTES
For cobweb felting, netting is laid both beneath and on top of the laid out wool tops to protect the delicate nature of the fine fibers. Make sure the netting you use is wide enough to fold over the top to encase the scarf, or use two pieces of netting.

When wetting down the laid out wool tops, you will need to use a finer spray bottle for dispensing the soapy water solution.

METHOD

LAYING OUT THE WOOL TOPS

1. Lay the wool onto a piece of netting that has been laid on top of a bamboo mat. Mark out an area approximately 15¾ x 39 in. (40 cm x 1 m) and start by laying out the two large lily shapes in candy pink. Fill in some of the petals with a mixture of red, white, and dark olive. Add the other random petals around the flowers in the same colors. The fibers you pull off and lay out should be very fine and sheer so that you can see through them, but they should all touch and overlap a little so they can bond together.

2. Now start to fill in the areas between the flowers using primarily pale turquoise mixed with some bright yellow and white here and there. Finish the outer edges with dark olive, leaving one side mostly just pale turquoise.

3. Around the very edge, place small, fine red dots of wool about 4¾–6 in. (12–15 cm) apart, half on the scarf and half off.

FELTING THE SCARF

1. Cover your laid out design with a second piece of netting, spray down with soapy water until completely wet through and roll up tightly in the bamboo mat. Roll back and forth about 500 times. If this seems arduous, split into five lots of 100 and take a breather in between!

2. Unroll the mat and gently remove the scarf from the netting, taking great care not to distort it as you pull it away. Rinse gently under lukewarm water, and wring gently.

3. Continue to roll the scarf in the bamboo mat, completing a full roll (with rotations) on both sides (see Simple Flat Felt, step 13, page 123), or stop when you have reached the desired shrinkage.

4. Rinse again to remove all traces of soap (use either lukewarm water, or extremes of hot and cold for more shrinkage) and then repeat the rolling process. The scarf will have shrunk by approximately 20%. Leave flat to dry.

FITTING THE SCARF

1. Try the scarf on to find where the ends meet naturally around your neck.

2. Make a small slit towards one end and feed the other end through the slit to keep the scarf in place.

3. The wool shouldn't fray, but you could add some decorative stitching around the opening to make it less fluffy.

Cobweb felting is achieved by laying out very small quantities of wool in just one or two very fine layers resembling a fine cobweb.

The scarf is not regular in shape and has been designed to be slightly wider at one end on purpose.

✦✦✦✦✦✦✦✦✦✦✦✦✦✦✦✦✦✦

The secret to a delicately draping scarf is not to use too much fiber when laying out the wool.

✦✦✦✦✦✦✦✦✦✦✦✦✦✦✦✦✦✦

A FELTED SPECTACLE GLASSES CASE

❖◆❖◆❖◆❖◆❖◆❖◆❖◆❖◆❖◆❖◆❖◆❖◆❖◆❖

Keep your reading glasses safe and snug with this fun case. Made from two layers of wool worked around a plastic template, the basic black glasses shape is wet felted into the outer layer, while the rest of the design—including the eyes—are needle felted on afterward, which allows for fine detailing to be added. The finishing touches of rhinestone "bling" are attached at the very end with some little dabs of glue.

MATERIALS

◆◆◆◆◆◆◆◆◆◆◆◆◆◆◆◆◆◆◆

MERINO WOOL TOPS

1½ oz (40 g) each of peppermint green, and salmon pink
Small amounts of bright red, black, white,
kingfisher blue, and racing green

OTHER REQUIREMENTS

Wet felting essentials (see page 116)
Strong template plastic
38-gauge felting needle and foam
Strong fabric glue
Small stick-on gems
Velcro, magnetic, or snap closure (optional)

Finished size: 5 x 8½ in. (13 x 22 cm)

TECHNIQUES
3-D SEAMLESS OBJECTS
(PAGE 124),
NEEDLE FELTING
(PAGE 134)

METHOD

WET FELTING THE GLASSES CASE SHAPE

1. First cut a template from strong template plastic making it 20% larger than you'd like your glasses case to be to allow for shrinkage. I used a rectangle about 7 x10½ in. (18 x 27 cm) and slightly rounded the corners at the base.

2. Working from the inner layer out, lay out the peppermint wool overlapping the edges of the template. Cover with netting, wet, soap and rub for a few minutes. Turn the template over and fold in the edges. Repeat on the other side.

3. Now lay down the outer layer of salmon pink with the fibers facing in the opposite direction, and overlap the edges. Add some fine wisps of black wool for the main frame of the glasses in the center. Keep the shape of the glasses fairly large within the space, but leave a little room around the edges. Try to keep the outline as neat and tidy as you can at this stage, although it can be added to later on when adding the needle felting details.

4. Cover, wet, soap and rub for about 10–20 minutes or until all the fibers are securely attached together. Turn over and fold in the edges.

5. Now you are working on the final side, so no overlap is required. Simply fill in the center with some more salmon pink, although if you want to you can add a little black heart to decorate. Repeat the rubbing until everything feels attached together.

6. Briefly rinse in lukewarm water, then do a complete roll on both sides (see 3-d Seamless Objects, step 9, page 127). Rinse in very hot water and briefly roll again.

7. Using small sharp scissors, cut the case open at one end and remove the template. Trim to neaten if necessary, and then soap, rub and felt the edges.

8. Remove all traces of soap with a hot rinse followed by a freezing cold rinse. Repeat the rolling on both sides until you are happy with the amount of shrinkage. Leave to dry.

NEEDLE FELTING THE FINE DETAILS

1. Insert some protective foam into the opening of the glasses case. Following the photographs opposite and below, begin by needle felting a red border around the black glasses frame, and finish with a very fine black line on the outer edge. Now add a very fine white line on the inside to define the lenses.

2. Make the eyes by using small amounts of white wool; add black eyelids and blue/green irises, with a tiny black dot in the center of each for the pupil.

FINISHING THE CASE

1. Add the stick-on gems at the top of each side of the glasses frame. Dab each gem with a dot of glue and use tweezers to position, then leave to dry.

2. To add a closure, sew in Velcro spots or a press stud on the inside, near the opening.

ROSE AND DAISY CORSAGES

✦ ✦

Adorn, embellish and accessorize with gorgeous felt flowers made in the colors of your choosing. These floral corsages look great in your hair, on the lapel of your coat, or on a bag. I have used them time and again to add the perfect finishing touch to the projects featured in this book.

TECHNIQUES
SIMPLE FLAT FELT (PAGE 120),
NEEDLE FELTING (PAGE 134)

MATERIALS

✦ ✦ ✦ ✦ ✦ ✦ ✦ ✦ ✦ ✦ ✦ ✦ ✦ ✦ ✦ ✦ ✦

MERINO WOOL TOPS

$^2/_3$ oz (20 g) each of two different colors of your choice for each rose or daisy plus small amounts for highlights if required and for the daisy centers (see notes) Small amounts of green for leaves

OTHER REQUIREMENTS

Wet felting essentials (see page 116)
38-gauge felting needle and foam

Finished size: between 3–5 in. (7.5–12 cm) in diameter

NOTES

To make a rose, you will need to make a rectangle of felt for each one in your desired colorway. Choosing two variations of the same color will result in the most realistic looking rose, such as bright red and cherry red, or pale pink and salmon pink.

Daisies are also cut from rectangles of felt using two variations of the same color. Layer the daisies so that the different colors, from each side of the felt you've made, can be seen.

METHOD

MAKING A ROSE

1. Taking one of your chosen colors, lay the wool out directly onto a waterproof surface to form a rectangle about 12 x 8 in. (30 x 20 cm) with all the fibers running in the same direction. Now add a fine layer of the second color on top in the opposite direction. Finish by adding highlights or lowlights of different colors around the very edges.

2. Cover with netting, wet down with soapy water, remove excess water with a cloth, add further soap, and rub each side well for about 10 minutes. Remove the netting and rinse briefly under lukewarm water.

3. Roll in a bamboo mat, 20 times in each direction on both sides as described on page 123 (see Simple Flat Felt, steps 12 and 13). Rinse again in very hot then very cold water, to remove all the soap. Repeat the rolling and then leave to dry.

4. Cut off the very outside of the felt rectangle in one continuous piece no more than 1 in. (2.5 cm) deep (see photo below left).

5. From the remaining felt, cut two wavy but vaguely circular shapes about 3 in. (7.5 cm) in diameter. Place one on top of the other.

6. Loosely coil the cut off edging strip (see photo below) and place on top of the circular shapes with the uncut edge uppermost.

7. Needle felt the coil onto the circular shapes, stabbing the needle through the base of the coil; work your way around from the outside to the center (see photo opposite).

8. Once the coil is held fast, sew tiny stitches around the base of the coil using a matching thread. Again, start at the outside and work your way to the center.

SCULPTING THE ROSE

4.

6.

9. Needle felt the petals further to add more dimension—you can sculpt their shape by needling at the base of each.

10. Small leaves are made using a piece of flat green felt. The leaf shapes are simply cut out and sewn to the back of the rose if required.

TIP
Using the felting needle at the base of the coil will help make the rose petals protrude backward and outward, and will shape the rose to make it look more realistic.

MAKING A DAISY

1. Make rectangles of flat felt in the same way as for the rose, steps 1–3.

2. Cut a circle for each daisy the size you want your corsage to be. For an eight-petalled daisy, use a pair of small, sharp scissors to make snips at 12, 3, 6 and 9 o'clock. Then make further snips in between so you have eight snips in total at regular intervals. Now round off the corner of each snip to create petals. You can adapt this technique to make daisies with more or fewer petals.

3. Make the center of the flower in one of the following ways: make a felt ball (see page 133), slice in half and glue in place; needle felt some wool to produce a raised bump; sew on a contrasting button.

4. For a "double" daisy, simply cut two circles of different colored felt of varying diameters, and cut the petals. Sit one on top of the other and secure with the center of your choice.

Follow my instructions in step 2 for the easiest way to make your daisy petals look even and neat.

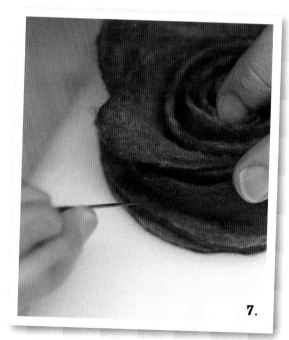

7.

CONTRARY MARY'S GARDEN SLIPPERS

❖❖❖❖❖❖❖❖❖❖❖❖❖❖❖❖❖❖❖❖❖❖❖❖

Bounce softly around your pad in this warm, enveloping, floral footwear.
The slippers are made around polystyrene lasts (forms) to fit your shoe size. As they are
finished in the washing machine, they are slightly easier on the time and effort scale!
You can make them either as mules, as shown, or booties, and adorn them with flowers
and needle felted details.

TECHNIQUES
USING A SHOE LAST
(PAGE 128),
SIMPLE FLAT FELT
(PAGE 120),
NEEDLE FELTING
(PAGE 134)

MATERIALS

❖❖❖❖❖❖❖❖❖❖❖❖❖❖❖❖❖❖

MERINO WOOL TOPS

3 oz (75 g) of racing green for the inner layer
3 oz (75 g) of dark olive for the middle layer
3 oz (75 g) of mid olive for the outer layer
1 oz (25 g) of custard yellow and $1/2$ oz (15 g) each of gold
and orange for the daffodils
Small amounts of red, candy pink, lilac, dusty mauve,
grass green, dark olive, bright yellow, rose pink,
citrus green, black, and white

OTHER REQUIREMENTS

Wet felting essentials (see page 116)
Pair of polystyrene shoe lasts in the appropriate size
Two plastic bags big enough to cover the lasts
Two elastic bands
Multicolored yarn (optional)
38-gauge felting needle and foam
Strong fabric glue
Sheepskin insoles (optional)
Slipper soles (see notes)

NOTES

The merino wool tops given are for an adult women's size $7^{1}/_{2}$–$8^{1}/_{2}$
and should be increased or decreased depending on your size.

To prolong the life of your slippers, finish with a sensible sole.
I prefer Regia slipper soles, as they have a foam layer built in,
which makes the slippers really comfy (see Resources, page 142).

METHOD

WET FELTING THE SLIPPERS

1. First prepare the shoe lasts (see Using a Shoe Last, step 1, page 128). Now prepare the wool tops: split each 1²⁄₃ oz (75 g) length in half to give two equal lengths—one for each foot. Split each length again into three equal lengths, one for the sole, one for the left side of the slipper and one for the right side.

2. Using the prepared lengths of racing green wool tops first, and working on one foot at a time, lay down and work the inner layer (see Using a Shoe Last, steps 2 and 3, pages 128–129). Start with the sole, then add each side, making sure that the entire last is covered including the very top.

3. Using the dark olive lengths next, lay down and work the middle layer in the same way.

4. Using the mid olive lengths, lay and work the outer layer but before rubbing the two sides, add a few background details first. I added a few stems in different greens and some smaller flowers using reds and pinks. Take care not to use the wool too thickly. When rubbing this time, you will need to work at it for about 30 minutes on each foot or until all the designs and fibers have firmly matted together.

5. Remove the netting and spend plenty of time rubbing both feet using soap, so you don't dislodge any of the designs. Once you are confident the designs have felted together really well, put the slippers in a washing machine on a 140°F (60°C) wash cycle. Add a pair of old jeans (or similar) to the wash to facilitate the felting process.

TRIMMING AND FITTING THE SLIPPERS

1. Remove the lasts (see step 5, page 129) and trim the slippers to your desired shape. For booties, trim away the top of each slipper and make a cut down the front too, making sure you can remove the lasts and get your feet in and out. For mules, leave a "cup" for the heel at the back of each slipper. Use pins to mark out the cutting lines and err on the side of caution—it's better to cut away gradually rather than ending up with too much missing! Leave to dry.

2. Check the fit. If the slippers are a little roomy, add some cozy sheepskin insoles. If they are really large, try taking a bath wearing them (you may want to lock the door to avoid embarrassment). Take care not to over-shrink them, as extremes of temperature and soap will reduce them in size quite dramatically. Be sure to remove all traces of soap. Once the lasts have been removed, do not put them back in the washing machine as this will result in disaster!

3. To finish off the cut edges, you could oversew them with a thick multicolored yarn.

MAKING THE DAFFODIL EMBELLISHMENTS

1. Following the instructions on page 120, make a piece of flat felt using two layers of custard yellow with a fine layer of gold over the top. Add a strip of orange down one side wide enough for the daffodil centers.

2. Referring to Making a Daisy, page 25, cut four flower petals from the custard yellow section, each with six shortish, well-rounded petals to resemble daffodil petals. Now cut two orange pieces from the edge, measuring about 1 x 4¾ in. (2.5 x 12 cm). You are going to use these pieces with the uncut edge uppermost.

3. To make the stamens, gather some very small amounts of orange, green, and gold. Make about six (three for each foot). Roll each one into a very fine strand about 2¾–3⅛ in. (7–8 cm) long (see Making a Handle/Strand, page 130).

4. Attach two yellow petal shapes onto the front of each slipper, slightly off-setting each one on top of the other. You can do this by needle felting, sewing or sticking with strong fabric glue (or a combination of these). Take an orange felt piece and with the uncut edge uppermost, needle felt the very base round into a circle in the center of the petals, overlapping the ends slightly. Add a few drops of strong fabric glue too, to secure.

5. Thread each stamen through a needle and sew down through the middle of the flower and up in a different place. If necessary, secure inside the slipper with a few small blobs of glue.

For mules, leave a "cup" for the heel at the back of each slipper.

✦✦✦✦✦✦✦✦✦✦✦✦✦✦✦✦✦✦✦✦

NEEDLE FELTING THE DETAILS

1. Now it's simply a case of getting creative with your needle felting, using more wool tops to make flat and raised designs on the front of the slippers. Add delphiniums with lilac and dusty mauve, and poppies using reds with black centers. Add a few more pink, orange, and white flowers too. (You can always use up any leftover colors that you have for the needle felting embellishments as you only need little bits.)

2. To make a ladybug, needle an oval of bright red in place, add a black head, two small white eyes and some small black spots on the ladybug's back.

TIP

Needle felted details are not quite as "hardy" as wet felted bits; to extend the life of your slippers for as long as possible, periodically stab them with a felting needle. Alternatively, wet felt the flowers on as part of the design, adding the shapes and colors over the top of the outer layer.

✦✦✦✦✦✦✦✦✦✦✦✦✦✦✦✦✦✦✦✦

CARNIVAL CARRY ALL BAG

◈ ◈

Make this fun brightly colored bag to carry all your bits and pieces in.
The flap keeps the things inside secure and the bamboo handle finishes it off nicely.
The bag is wet felted around a plastic template using some pre-felted shapes for the daisies,
and then it is finished with some needle felting afterward.

MATERIALS

◆ ◆ ◆ ◆ ◆ ◆ ◆ ◆ ◆ ◆ ◆ ◆ ◆ ◆ ◆ ◆

MERINO WOOL TOPS

3 oz (75 g) of lime green for the inner layer
3 oz (75 g) of pale turquoise for
the middle layer
3 oz (75 g) of Turquoise Treasure wool blend
for the outer layer (see page 142)
1 oz (25 g) of Fairy Floss Fantazia wool blend
for the large circle designs (see page 142)
Small amounts of black, white, red, cherry red,
orange, and kingfisher blue

OTHER REQUIREMENTS

Wet felting essentials (see page 116)
Strong template plastic
38-gauge felting needle and foam
Pre-felt, small amounts of orange and red
Bamboo handle 9½ in. (24 cm) wide
Snap or magnetic closure (optional)

Finished size: 13¾ x 12½ in. (35 x 32 cm) with flap closed

TECHNIQUES
3-D SEAMLESS OBJECTS
(PAGE 124),
NEEDLE FELTING
(PAGE 134)

METHOD

WET FELTING THE BAG

1. Cut a piece of strong template plastic measuring 23³/₄ x 14¹/₂ in. (60 x 37 cm). This is bigger than the finished item will be as the felt will shrink.

2. Lay out a layer of lime green horizontally, overlapping the edges of the template. Cover with netting, wet, soap and rub for a few minutes. Turn the template over and fold in the edges. Repeat on the other side to complete the inner layer.

3. For the middle layer, repeat step 2 using the pale turquoise, but lay the wool in the opposite direction—vertically—remembering to fold in the seam overlap each time you turn.

4. For the first side of the outer layer, lay the Turquoise Treasure blend horizontally allowing for a larger than normal overlap.

5. Now add the pattern. Create some large pink circles using the Fairy Floss Fantazia and outline these with a little cherry red. (I did one half off the side, so that I could continue it around on the other side in step 7.) Add a black center with a white edge and then place a pre-felt shape in the middle—I used orange daisies. Add a small dot of red wool in the center. Cut petals from orange and red pre-felt, and place five of these around each large pink circle.

6. Cover, wet, soap and rub for about 20–30 minutes, or until all the fibers are securely attached together. Turn over and fold in the edges.

7. Now working on the final side, lay down the Turquoise Treasure blend, but remember not to overlap the edges this time. Add the pattern as in step 5. Cover, wet, soap and rub for another 20–30 minutes or so.

8. Rinse briefly in warm water, then do a complete roll on both sides as described on page 127 (see 3-d Seamless Objects, step 9). Rinse under very hot water, then roll briefly again.

9. Carefully cut open along the top of the bag and remove the template.

MAKING THE BAG FLAP

1. Now think about where the designs are placed and decide on the size of the flap you'd like; cut away the felt on the other side of the new flap.

2. Fold over the newly formed flap and cut the scalloped edge, using pins as a guide to space the scallops evenly. Soap, rub and felt the newly cut edges.

3. Rinse again using very hot then very cold water, making sure all traces of soap are removed. Roll again until you are happy with the shrinkage. Leave to dry.

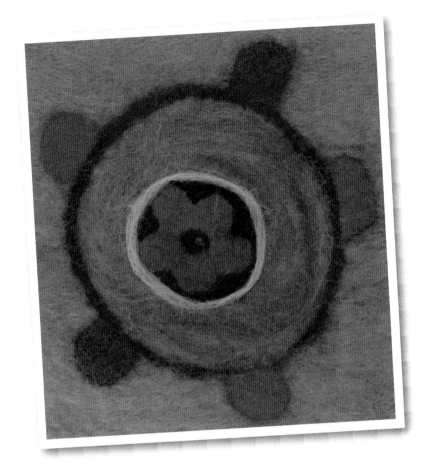

NEEDLE FELTING THE DETAILS

1. Use a mix of red and Fairy Floss Fantazia to needle felt around the scalloped edge to make it really stand out.

2. I also added a tiny dot of kingfisher blue to the center of each daisy motif.

ATTACHING THE HANDLE

1. Attach the handle on the inside of the flap using a matching embroidery thread. Use the fibrous nature of the felt to "hide" the stitches to prevent them from showing on the outside.

2. Add a snap or magnetic closure (or something similar) if you want your bag to stay shut.

Secure the bamboo handle to the inside of the bag flap with a matching embroidery thread.

✦ ✦ ✦ ✦ ✦ ✦ ✦ ✦ ✦ ✦ ✦ ✦ ✦ ✦ ✦ ✦ ✦ ✦

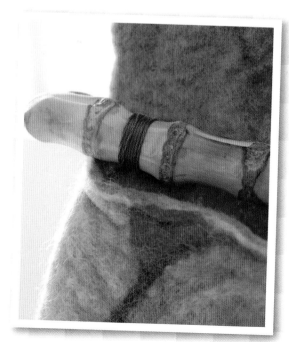

PRETTY THINGS FOR YOUR HOME

BANQUETING BUNTING

◆◆◆◆◆◆◆◆◆◆◆◆◆◆◆◆◆◆◆◆◆◆◆◆◆◆◆◆

Let the party begin by hanging this flowery bunting as decoration for your own mini carnival. Made very simply from one long rectangle of flat felt cut into pennants and strung from giant ric rac, this is a straightforward project that is guaranteed to raise a smile and possibly even a glass and a cheer!

MATERIALS

◆◆◆◆◆◆◆◆◆◆◆◆◆◆◆◆◆◆

MERINO WOOL TOPS

2 oz (50 g) each of white, sage green, pale blue,
and custard yellow
⅖ oz (20 g) of pale turquoise
Small amounts of red, lilac, purple,
candy pink, cerise, orange, olive green,
yellow, mid mauve, peach, emerald green,
lime green, and other colors
of your choosing for flower details

TECHNIQUES
SIMPLE FLAT FELT
(PAGE 120),
MAKING A BALL
(PAGE 133)

OTHER REQUIREMENTS

Wet felting essentials (see page 116)
Some wool nepps and Angelina glitter fiber (optional)
2 yd (1.8 m) giant rickrack
Strong fabric glue

Finished size: about 3⅛ yd (3 m) long with pennants 10 in. (25 cm) high

NOTES

The felt piece from which the pennants will be cut is made as a very long rectangle that is "mirrored" top and bottom. By using white along the top and the bottom edges and the blue-green/flowers in the middle, there is no wastage when you cut the triangular pennants and ALL the felt is used.

The felt piece is about 13¾ in. x 2 yd (35 cm x 1.8 m) when first laid out, but it will shrink to about 10¼ x 59 in. (26 cm x 1.5 m) when finished.

I have added a few strands of Angelina glitter fiber in Aurora Borealis to give a little extra sparkle to the bunting.

METHOD

MAKING THE FELT

1. Start by laying out the background fibers straight onto a waterproof surface. Lay out a band of sage green about 6 in. (15 cm) high and 70 in. (1.8 m) wide. Add a 2 in. (5 cm) high band of pale blue both above and below the sage green, and follow this with a 2 in. (5 cm) high band of white both above and below the pale blue. Try to blend the background colors into one another as you lay them down, adding wispy amounts over and over so the lines going from one color to another aren't too hard. Adding a small amount of light turquoise in between the sage green and the pale blue helps the blending a little. You can lay the wool in any direction, ideally finishing with it lying horizontally. The wool should be fairly thick if you want to avoid bunting that is too thin and wispy.

2. If you choose to, you can sprinkle a few strands of Angelina glitter fiber over the wool. It is important not to use too much and to make sure you lay very wispy amounts of wool over the top of it. This will ensure that when the fibers felt together the Angelina gets trapped in place and doesn't fall off (see Simple Flat Felt, step 5, page 121).

3. Now start to add the flower details. It is really important not to use too much wool if you want delicate looking flowers. The less wool you use, the more realistic they will be—you really hardly need any at all, and keep it wispy! To make a foxglove, create a very fine dark green stem, then some tiny lilac blobs that sit randomly down the stem. Add poppies here and there using a small circle of bright red with a black center. Add a few pink flowers with yellow centers. You can add texture and interest with a few wool nepps if you choose to, but remember to trap them in with a little bit of wispy wool over the top.

4. Once you are happy with your design, wet felt together (see Simple Flat Felt, page 120).

MAKING THE BUNTING

1. Once the felt is dry it can be cut into pennants. Start by pinning out the lines of the flags BEFORE you cut, starting from the top to the bottom to avoid wastage and to use all the felt.

2. Sew the cut out flags onto the giant rickrack trim and decorate in between the pennants with little felt flowers. You can either create some flat felt flowers from leftover pieces, or wet felt a few small squares to cut them from. I used pink/purple colors for my flowers, with yellow balls (cut in half) for the centers. Refer to Rose and Daisy Corsages, page 22, for how to make a daisy, and Making a Ball, page 133, for making a flower center.

Make the daisy centers by cutting each felt ball in half and placing them in between each pennant at the top of the bunting.

Flowers made from flat felt are
used to trim between the
pennants at the top of the
bunting and are added at the
very end.

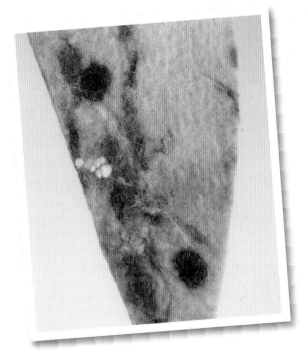

When laying down the wet felt
flowers, make the stems and
flowers go up and down so that
they aren't facing in any
particular direction.

LIGHTHEARTED LAMPSHADE

◆◆◆◆◆◆◆◆◆◆◆◆◆◆◆◆◆◆◆◆◆◆◆◆◆◆◆◆◆◆◆

Using a medley of different colors and patterns, you can transform an old lampshade frame into a carousel of light. Made from eight panels of flat felt, my lampshade is pieced together using brightly colored ribbons, then accented with flowers and even more ribbons to add the finishing touch.

**TECHNIQUES
SIMPLE FLAT FELT
(PAGE 120)**

MATERIALS

◆◆◆◆◆◆◆◆◆◆◆◆◆◆◆◆◆

MERINO WOOL TOPS
2 oz (50 g) of white
1 oz (25 g) each of lilac, peppermint green,
pale blue, pale pink, custard yellow, and peach
⅔ oz (20 g) each of pale pink, sage green,
light turquoise, and candy pink
Small amounts of peppermint green, gold, peach,
bright rose pink, pale olive yellow, dark green,
white, lilac, bright yellow, cherry red, salmon pink,
dark duck egg, dusty pink, maroon, bright red, and pale blue

OTHER REQUIREMENTS
Wet felting essentials (see page 116)
Lampshade frame (see notes)
Eight felt roses and daisies (see notes)
¼ in. (5 mm) wide ribbons (see notes)
Black pom-pom trim (optional)

Finished size: each panel 17¼ x 9 in. (44 x 23 cm)

NOTES
This lampshade uses an eight-panel frame but you can easily adapt the instructions to suit any frame. Each panel is made from a different piece of felt each decorated with a different design. The panels are sewn together using ribbons, each a little longer than the lampshade height and left to hang at the base.

To trim the re-covered frame, I have used a selection of roses and daisies (see Rose and Daisy Corsages, page 22).

METHOD

◆◆◆◆◆◆◆◆◆◆◆◆◆◆◆◆◆◆◆◆◆◆◆◆◆◆◆◆

PREPARATIONS TO BE MADE BEFORE YOU START

1. It is really important to measure each panel of your lampshade frame accurately and then lay out the wool tops at least 25% larger to allow for shrinkage. It doesn't matter if the felt panels are slightly too big, as they can be trimmed afterward if necessary, but it obviously does matter if they are too small!

2. When laying out the wool, you can work onto a piece of netting on top of a bamboo mat, or directly onto a flat waterproof surface.

PANEL 1: PALE BLUE WITH WHITE SPOTS

1. Having calculated the size you require, lay out a rectangle of pale blue with all the fibers facing in the same direction. Make the layer of wool relatively sheer, making sure there are no holes. There should be a fine even coverage (see tip).

2. Now lay the white spots on top of the blue. It's really important not to use too much wool—coil the wool round into circles, but make sure the circles are flat and sheer so that they will rub together easily.

3. Wet, soap and rub, making sure as you work that your designs stay where you intended them to be (see Simple Flat Felt, step 9, page 122). Rub and roll the felt until it is the correct size: keep checking to see how much the panel has shrunk, bearing in mind the size of your lampshade frame. After the final rinsing you can continue to shrink it further by rolling if necessary until it reaches the optimum size.

4. Leave to dry, and iron flat with a cool iron.

PANEL 2: WHITE WITH PINK PEONIES

1. Start by laying out a rectangle of white wool tops, using very small quantities of wool.

2. Lay large bright pink circles at random. Accent these with darker pink lines to indicate petals. Make the centers with pale olive yellow and green wool, and add cherry red highlights. Make the stems with the sage green, curling them around slightly. Add a cherry red highlight down the side of each stem. Add small leaves along the stems using sage green, adding a darker green edging and vein down each center.

3. Felt together as Panel 1, steps 3 and 4.

PANEL 3: LILAC AND GREEN TRELLIS WITH GOLD DAISIES

1. Start with a base layer of lilac wool. Add a fine peppermint green trellis over the top. Pull long lengths of wool and gently tease out to make longer and finer. Lay diagonally in one direction first, then the other, to create the diamond crisscross pattern.

2. Now lay out the gold daisies on top, highlighting the center of each petal with a sage green inner. Make a peach colored center for each daisy, and in the very center, add a little pale pink, plus a few tiny multicolored dots in the middle to indicate stamens.

3. Felt together as Panel 1, steps 3 and 4.

PANEL 4: GREEN WITH FLYING FLOWERS

1. Lay out a peppermint green background adding lilac spots at random.

2. Next create the bright turquoise circles for the flowers, adding a candy pink and red middle to each and a gold center. Create a pair of bright green leaf shapes and "tuck" behind the flower; outline with a little dark green.

3. Felt together as Panel 1, steps 3 and 4.

PANEL 5: PINK WITH HEART HOT AIR BALLOONS

1. Lay out a pale pink background. Create random hearts using a mixture of colors—I used bright pink, peach, turquoise, lilac, pale turquoise, peppermint green, and pale yellow olive. Outline the hearts with some bright red wool, adding a little red basket underneath each one.

2. Felt together as Panel 1, steps 3 and 4.

> **TIP**
> It might be worth doing a test panel first to get a feel for how much wool you need—which really isn't all that much! If you make the felt too thick, not much light will shine through.

◆◆◆◆◆◆◆◆◆◆◆◆◆◆◆◆◆◆◆◆◆◆

Panels 1 and 8.

❖ ❖ ❖ ❖ ❖ ❖ ❖ ❖ ❖ ❖ ❖ ❖ ❖ ❖ ❖ ❖

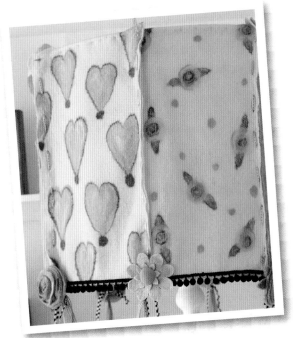

Panels 5 and 4.

❖ ❖ ❖ ❖ ❖ ❖ ❖ ❖ ❖ ❖ ❖ ❖ ❖ ❖ ❖ ❖

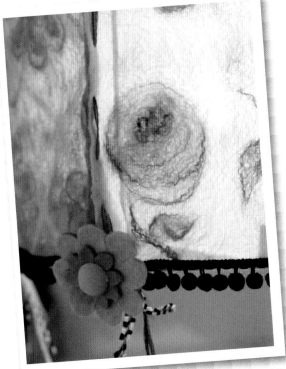

Panels 3 and 2.

❖ ❖ ❖ ❖ ❖ ❖ ❖ ❖ ❖ ❖ ❖ ❖ ❖ ❖ ❖ ❖ ❖

TIP
To give a more embellished look,
short ribbon lengths have been
used to trim the flowers at the
bottom of the panels.

❖ ❖ ❖ ❖ ❖ ❖ ❖ ❖ ❖ ❖ ❖ ❖ ❖ ❖ ❖ ❖

PANEL 6: CUSTARD YELLOW WITH PEACOCK EYES

1. Lay out a custard yellow background. Start to create salmon pink ovals at regular intervals to cover the panel. Now add a small green circle at the base of each oval. Outline the green circle with a dark duck egg outline and add a smaller "eye" of pale turquoise. Now outline each pink oval with cherry red.

2. Felt together as Panel 1, steps 3 and 4.

PANEL 7: WHITE WITH CLIMBING ROSES

1. Lay out a white background. Start by laying out the stems— I used a sage green with a dark green to highlight the side of each stem. Begin the roses with a large dusty pink blob, alternating where they sit on each stem. Add a few rosebud shapes too—like little egg shapes. Add highlights and details to the roses, using mostly maroon or cherry red. Use lines to indicate where the petals are, and make the gold middles slightly off center. Add pale pink highlights too, and some green bases to the rosebuds.

2. Now add some leaves. Use the same green as you used for the stems, and highlight using darker green around the outer edges and down the center veins.

3. Felt together as Panel 1, steps 3 and 4.

PANEL 8: PEACH WITH CHECKS AND FLOWERS

1. Lay out a peach background. Add small flecks of bright pink over the top.

2. Now create the checkered pattern, first laying pale pink lengths of wool horizontally, then vertically over the top, to form the crisscross pattern. Mimic this using first lime green horizontally and then pale blue vertically, off-setting each color so you can still see the pink beneath.

3. Add flowers all over the background at random. For each flower, lay a ring of five small cherry red circles to indicate the petals and one circle to the center. Add a pale yellow center to the middle of each circle, and a dark rose pink surround.

4. Felt together as Panel 1, steps 3 and 4.

TIP

The different panels have been designed to contrast with one another, but also to retain a sense of balance. Use trimmings and flowers to help tie the panel designs together.

✦✦✦✦✦✦✦✦✦✦✦✦✦✦✦✦✦✦✦✦✦✦

PIECING THE PANELS AND COVERING THE FRAME

1. The easiest way to piece the panels together is to first pin them around each upright and around the top and bottom of the frame, so that you can keep adjusting them until they fit together snugly.

2. Once you are happy with the fit, fold the edges over the top of the frame and baste in place.

3. Using a length of ribbon threaded through a large-eyed needle and starting at the top of the frame with a knot, begin to sew the panels together one by one with the seam facing outward. Use a long decorative running stitch and leave the remaining ribbon hanging at the base. Add further small lengths of ribbon to form a bunch at the end of the seam.

4. Once all the panels are in place, securely sew the top around the frame and remove the original basting stitch holding it all in place. Repeat around the base.

ADDING THE TRIMMINGS

1. Add the black pom-pom trim around the bottom of the lampshade if desired.

2. Add a felt flower at the base of each panel seam, on top of the hanging ribbon ends. I have alternated felt roses with daisies.

Panels 7 and 6.

To make the raised centers of the
flat flowers, make and cut a felt
ball in half and glue in place.

QUEEN OF HEARTS CUSHION

❖❖❖❖❖❖❖❖❖❖❖❖❖❖❖❖❖❖❖❖❖❖❖❖

By felting onto a very sheer fabric (nuno felting) you can create some wonderful effects
as the material ruffles together when the wool shrinks. By leaving areas free of wool
you can see through the fabric to create the little embroidered pocket clouds on this heavenly
heart-shaped cushion. Adorn with a single red rose.

MATERIALS

◆◆◆◆◆◆◆◆◆◆◆◆◆◆◆◆◆◆◆

MERINO WOOL TOPS

½ oz (15 g) each of pale blue, pale turquoise,
sage green, citrus, and mid olive
Small amounts of cherry red, turquoise,
dusty mauve, lilac, candy pink, orange,
gold, red, black, cerise, dark olive,
racing green, and white

*TECHNIQUES
SIMPLE FLAT FELT
(PAGE 120)*

OTHER REQUIREMENTS

Wet felting essentials (see page 116)
One 22 in. (55 cm) square pale-colored silk chiffon (see notes)
Two 22 in. (55 cm) squares ready-made white felt
Heart-shaped cushion pad about 12 in. (30 cm) wide (or stuffing)
48 in. (1.2 m) pink pom-pom trim
Blue and red embroidery threads
One felt rose with leaves (see page 22)

Finished size: approximately 12 in. (30 cm) at widest point

NOTES

For nuno felting, you will need to choose an appropriate fabric that
has a large enough weave to accept the wool fibers through it. Any
fabric with an open weave—such as chiffon, organza or cheesecloth
(muslin)—is suitable for this technique.

METHOD

MAKING THE NUNO PANEL

1. The secret to creating the delicate effect is to very finely lay out the wool onto the chiffon (or similar gauzy fabric) panel, so that it remains very lightweight and has a chance to attach to the fabric without felting too quickly. Starting with the background, lay fine wisps of pale blue at the top, blending down through the pale turquoise into the sage green and citrus, and ending up with the mid olive at the base. Leave a couple of areas in the sky free of fibers so that the chiffon shows through (to be sewn around and filled with stuffing later).

2. On top of the background layer, lay out a small butterfly in cherry red with a turquoise center. For the flowers, use very small amounts of lilac and dusty mauve in small blobs running down a stem of dark olive,

alongside the same in candy pink, and another in cerise and red. Lay out a few poppies using bright red and cherry red, adding tiny black centers. Add some more bits of color for a suggestion of other flowers—a small amount of gold or orange looks good.

3. Once you are happy with your design, cover with netting and wet down with cool soapy water. (It's important that the water isn't too hot, as you don't want to felt this piece too quickly.) Make sure you use plenty of soap as you start to rub the piece together. Gradually the wool will start to attach itself to the fabric, and the little fibers will felt through to the other side and grab onto it. Keep rubbing until this happens—20–30 minutes should suffice for a piece this size.

4. Once the fibers are well attached to the fabric, rinse briefly in lukewarm water and roll in a bamboo mat (see Simple Flat Felt, steps 12 and 13, page 123). This should start to shrink the wool fibers and the piece will get a little smaller.

5. Rinse again in hot water and then cold, to remove all traces of soap; then roll again. Keep in mind that you want the piece to fit your cushion front, so don't shrink too much; the piece should now have shrunk quite significantly and will feel well felted. Leave to dry.

MAKING THE CUSHION COVER

1. Measure and cut two pieces of white felt about ¾ in. (2 cm) bigger than the cushion pad all the way around. Use one of these as a template to cut the nuno panel to the same shape and size.

2. Outline the butterfly in red running stitch. Stitch the body with blue thread, and sew the antennae in red, finishing with French knots.

3. Put the nuno panel wrong sides together with one of the white felt hearts and insert a little white wool tops into the cloud areas. Sew a simple running stitch in pale blue around the edge of the clouds to make them stand proud.

4. Place right sides together with the remaining white felt heart, pin and sew leaving a 6–8 in. (15–20 cm) opening.

5. Turn inside out, insert the cushion pad through the opening and hand-sew to close.

ADDING THE TRIMMINGS

1. Pin and sew the pink pom-pom trim all the way around the cushion.

2. Make a red rose using 29½ in. (75 cm) each of red and cherry red for the flower and 19¾ in. (50 cm) dark olive and mid olive for the leaves (see Rose and Daisy Corsages, page 22). Sew in place with small stitches and/or strong fabric glue.

Before sewing the cushion together, stuff a little white wool into the unfelted fabric clouds; use a running stitch around the edge to keep the wool in place.

❖ ❖ ❖ ❖ ❖ ❖ ❖ ❖ ❖ ❖ ❖ ❖ ❖ ❖ ❖ ❖ ❖ ❖ ❖

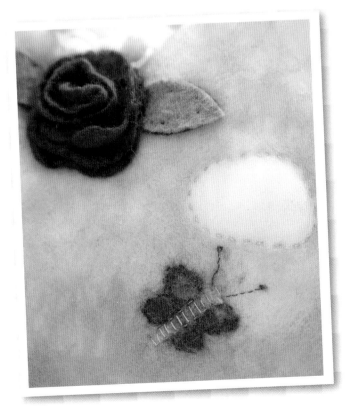

Outline the butterfly in a red running stitch and add antennae, finishing off with French knots. Using blue thread, sew some details down its center.

❖ ❖ ❖ ❖ ❖ ❖ ❖ ❖ ❖ ❖ ❖ ❖ ❖ ❖ ❖ ❖ ❖ ❖ ❖

BEWITCHING BUTTERFLY CURTAIN

✦✦✦✦✦✦✦✦✦✦✦✦✦✦✦✦✦✦✦✦✦✦✦✦✦✦

Using a sheer piece of fabric as a light ethereal base, needle felt these beautiful butterflies for a delicate window treatment. The final butterfly is wet felted and sewn on at the end to stand proud from the curtain. Adjust the length according to your needs.

TECHNIQUES
NEEDLE FELTING
(PAGE 134),
SIMPLE FLAT FELT
(PAGE 120)

MATERIALS

✦✦✦✦✦✦✦✦✦✦✦✦✦✦✦✦

MERINO WOOL TOPS
2 oz (50 g) of peppermint green
Small amounts of pale turquoise,
candy pink, bright rose pink, olive green,
yellow, and orange

OTHER REQUIREMENTS
Wet felting essentials (see page 116)
36- and 38-gauge felting needles and foam
Multi-needle tool (if desired)
Gauze-like fabric (see notes)

Finished size: see notes

NOTES
The minimum length of fabric required is 24 in. (60 cm).
You can make the curtain as long as you like, but do allow an extra
12 in. (30 cm) to the desired finished length for making the curtain
ties at the top. The width of the fabric will be determined by the
width of your window.

Select a fabric that has an open weave texture and that is sheer and
see-through, for example an organza, voile, chiffon or
similar—man-made or silk, it really doesn't matter.

METHOD

PREPARING YOUR FABRIC

1. Cut your chosen fabric to the size you require and if necessary hem the sides.

2. Using the template on page 136, trace the butterfly onto paper and cut out. Now lay the fabric in front of you and decide how many butterflies you want and where you want them to be positioned.

NEEDLE FELTING THE BUTTERFLIES

1. Place a block of protective foam underneath the fabric where you want to work your first butterfly. Place the paper template on top and using the peppermint green wool, start to needle felt a little wool around the edge of the shape to outline the butterfly. Now fill in the butterfly with the same color. You could use several felting needles in a multi-needle tool to make this a little quicker.

2. Using a small amount of pale turquoise, needle felt an edge to the butterfly and also the middle "line" of the wings. Add some olive green down the center for the body and outline this in pale turquoise too, adding antennae at the top. Add a tiny orange blob at the end of each antenna and some yellow stripes down the center of the body.

3. Referring to the photograph, add the candy pink spots to the wings, adding slightly smaller rose pink spots in the center of each.

4. Repeat until you have completed sufficient butterflies fluttering across your curtain!

WET FELTING A BUTTERFLY

1. Lay out the wool directly onto a waterproof surface, making the butterfly shape about 20% bigger than the butterfly template. Lay out the wool in exactly the same order as used for the needle felted butterflies, but you will need to use quite a bit more wool to ensure that this butterfly is a little thicker so that it doesn't flop when it is sewn onto the curtain. Shape the edges carefully so that they won't need to be trimmed once felted.

2. Wet felt the butterfly following the instructions for Simple Flat Felt, page 120. It is ready when it has shrunk to approximately the same size as the needle felted butterflies. Leave to dry.

3. Attach the finished butterfly to the curtain in your chosen position by sewing it in place around the body ONLY using a matching thread, leaving the wings to stand proud for a 3-d effect.

FINISHING THE CURTAIN

1. Working at the top edge, use a sharp pair of dressmaking scissors to cut the fabric to leave a long "tie" approximately every 3–5 in. (8–12 cm) along the width of the curtain. Now cut each tie into two down the center, so you can tie it around your curtain pole.

2. Depending on the fabric, you may want to hem the bottom edge, or simply fray it and leave it, as I have.

Using a fabric that looks effective when frayed saves hemming. By cutting into the fabric and creating long ties, the curtain can be quickly hung onto a curtain pole.

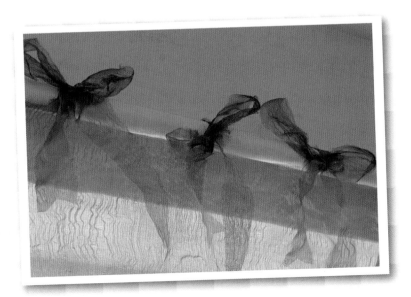

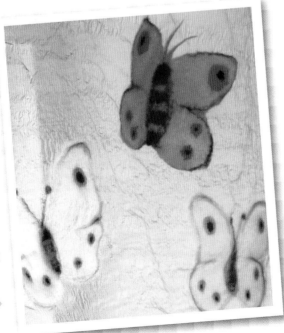

I needle felted four butterflies in place directly onto the fabric, and made a fifth wet felted butterfly to sew on.

LESSER SPOTTED FELTY WARBLER

Make this dinky woolly songbird to brighten up your mantelpiece or windowsill. He is simply made using sculptural needle felting, and his decorated wings and tail feathers are wet felted separately, then attached. Yarn-covered wire is used to make his sturdy little legs and feet.

MATERIALS

TECHNIQUES
NEEDLE FELTING
(PAGE 134),
SIMPLE FLAT FELT
(PAGE 120)

MERINO WOOL TOPS
1 oz (25 g) of pale turquoise
⅓ oz (10 g) each of lilac, sage, gold, candy pink,
rose pink, citrus, and lime green
Smaller amounts of candy pink, red, lilac,
pale yellow, black, white, dusty mauve,
orange, peppermint green,
pale yellow olive, and purple

OTHER REQUIREMENTS
Wet felting essentials (see page 116)
36- and 38-gauge felting needles and foam
Multi-needle tool
Strong fabric glue
20 in. (50 cm) of 18-gauge (0.9mm) galvanized wire and fine-nosed pliers
Multicolored yarn (see notes)

Finished size: 5½ x 4 in. (14 x 10 cm) including tail feathers

NOTES
To cover the wire legs and feet I chose a slubby textured wool:
Noro Kureyon Sock Yarn color S263.

METHOD

MAKING THE BODY

1. Using pale turquoise wool and the multi-needle tool with the larger 36-gauge needles, form the body. Refine the shape, adding more wool onto the head area, and gradually building the shape as you work. Keep needling into some areas to reduce the fibers down (see Sculptural Needle Felting, steps 1 and 2, page 135).

2. From now on use a slightly smaller 38-gauge needle. To make the beak, gather together a small ball of pale yellow wool and needle into shape. Add a tiny bit of orange to the tip and a fine black line down each side. Attach the beak by needling it in the center of the front of the head, making sure it is well attached at the sides. Add a little more pale yellow wool around the join if necessary.

3. Needle felt a round lilac eye on each side of the head, adding a red rim around the outside and a small black dot in the center. Add some pink and peppermint green spots on the front of the chest and some peppermint green, red and orange stripes on the back.

MAKING THE LEGS

1. Make each leg from a piece of wire approximately 4¾ in. (12 cm) long. Use fine-nosed pliers to bend the wire into a three-pronged foot shape. Start by folding the first "toe" in the center of the piece of wire (**A**), and continue to form the other two toes on either side of it (**B**). Twist the remaining wire together to form the leg (**C**). Bend the legs so that they stand up unaided to give the felty warbler the best chance to stand up too!

2. Leaving an area at the top of each leg free of wool, cover the legs and toes with the yarn, winding it around until all the wire is hidden, except the very ends of the toes which peep out like claws (**D**)!

3. Use a large 36-gauge felting needle to make two holes in the base of the bird's body just over halfway back. Experiment to find the point of balance. Keep adjusting and bending the legs until he stands up on his own. When you are happy, apply a little blob of glue into each hole, insert the legs and leave to dry.

MAKING THE WINGS

1. Make a piece of randomly colored felt using citrus, lime, rose, candy, pale yellow olive, gold, and lilac (see Simple Flat Felt, page 120). Alternatively, you could use your felt leftovers or ready-made felt.

2. Cut two wing shapes from the felt; needle or glue each one into place on either side of the bird.

MAKING THE TAIL

1. Cut the tail feathers from different colored areas of the felt. These can be decorated further by needle felting designs on top—I needled on some circles and stripes using citrus, pale turquoise, and purple.

2. Needle felt the feathers into position; the more you stab them in, the more they will sit up and come forward a little, so experiment until they look pert! Add a little dab of glue underneath the feathers to make sure they are secure.

MAKING THE LEGS

A.

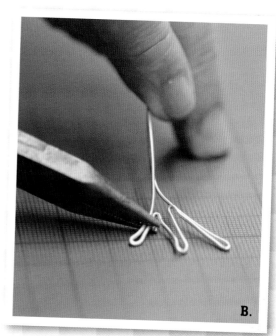

B.

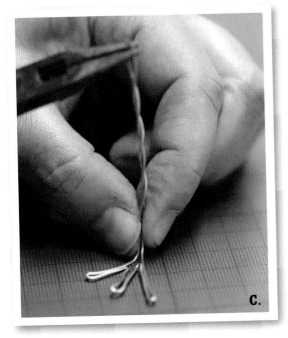

C.

D.

CROWNING GLORY CHANDELIER

❖❖❖❖❖❖❖❖❖❖❖❖❖❖❖❖❖❖❖❖❖❖❖❖❖

This magnificent felt centerpiece will take the limelight in any home! Use it with low energy, battery-powered LED lights—in and around it—to make it twinkle and sparkle on darker evenings. Based around a wire framework, this carnival-esque chandelier incorporates many aspects of feltmaking all together in one project.

MATERIALS

❖❖❖❖❖❖❖❖❖❖❖❖❖❖❖❖

MERINO WOOL TOPS

For full details of quantities and colors used for component parts see Method on the following page

OTHER REQUIREMENTS

Wet felting essentials (see page 116)
38-gauge felting needle and foam
Variegated chunky yarn
3¼ yd (3 m) of 12-gauge (2 mm) galvanized wire
5½ yd (5 m) of 18-gauge (0.9 mm) galvanized wire
Fine-nosed pliers and wire cutters
26-gauge (0.4 mm) craft (beading) wire
Selection of brightly colored buttons
Optional extras: selection of large glass and plastic beads,
five chandelier drops, five battery-powered plastic tea lights,
and a few feather butterflies

Finished size: approximately 51 x 27 in. (1.3 m x 70 cm)

TECHNIQUES
HANDLES AND STRANDS,
BEADS AND BALLS
(PAGE 130),
NEEDLE FELTING
(PAGE 134),
SIMPLE FLAT FELT
(PAGE 120),
3-D SEAMLESS OBJECTS
(PAGE 124)

NOTES

IMPORTANT If you intend using a bulb or a lamp within the chandelier, these must be LED or low energy so that they do not get hot to the touch and do not cause a fire hazard.

The variegated chunky yarn is used to cover the wire frame of the chandelier and also to supplement the felted hanging strands as necessary. I used Colinette One Zero in Lagoon.

METHOD

◆◆◆◆◆◆◆◆◆◆◆◆◆◆◆◆◆◆◆◆◆◆◆◆◆◆◆◆◆◆

MAKING THE FELT PIECES

Roses About 20–25 roses are required and these are made from a combination of brightly colored merino wool tops: candy pink, rose pink, citrus green, pale turquoise, pale pink, peach, lilac, dusty mauve, gold, custard yellow, red, and cherry red. For basic making instructions, see Rose and Daisy Corsages, page 22, but make larger pieces of felt so you can make several roses from each color. Vary the sizes slightly, and leave threads hanging at the back to tie them onto the chandelier.

Strands Make about 20 fine strands with a finished length of about 39–47 in. (1–1.2 m) following the instructions for Making a Handle/Strand, page 130. (Note, you will be able to make between 5 and 10 strands from about a 1 oz (25 g) length of wool, depending on the thickness of the strands.) Use a combination of brightly colored merino wool tops: bright yellow, candy pink, pale yellow olive, cherry red, bright red, black, white, peach, pale pink, jade, peppermint green, orange, lilac, citrus green, and turquoise. If the strands end up too short, they can be tied together and supplemented with the variegated chunky yarn.

Felt beads You will need about 30 beads. These are made from six or seven different felt sausages and sliced into rounds like cutting salami (see Making a Bead Sausage, page 132). Use a combination of brightly colored merino wool tops: bright yellow, black, white, pale blue, red, salmon pink, turquoise, orange, bright olive, rose pink, grass green, pale turquoise, and citrus green. (Note, you will need about 2 oz (50 g) of the colors used to wrap around the outside of each sausage, and smaller amounts for the middle.)

Small and medium felt balls You will need about 18 medium-sized balls approximately ¾ in. (2 cm) in diameter and about 15 small felt balls about ⅜ in. (1cm) in diameter, made from a combination of brightly colored merino wool tops: bright olive, bright yellow, red, kingfisher blue, candy pink, cherry red, turquoise, retro red, cerise, grass green, orange, and gold. (Note, a small felt ball requires only a few ounces/grams of wool, whereas a larger felt ball may need two or three times the amount; and you should remember that they can shrink down quite dramatically when felted.) See Making a Ball, steps 1 and 2, page 133.

Large felt balls In addition, make four large balls measuring approximately 2⅜ in. (6 cm) in diameter from merino wool tops in candy pink, rose pink, pale blue, cerise, and citrus green (for quantities, see note in step above). Decorate the finished balls with some needle felt designs, three with daisies using a combination of red, orange, turquoise, and green petals with black and white centers, and one with some turquoise spots with bright yellow outlines and candy pink centers.

Daisies You will need about 10 double daisies measuring about 3⅛–4 in. (8–10 cm) in diameter and about 15 smaller single daisies made from a combination of brightly colored merino wool tops: cerise, lilac, orange, pale turquoise, rose pink, citrus green, candy pink, bright yellow, cherry red, "phantasmagorical" blend, peach, jade, and gold. For how to make single and double daisies see Rose and Daisy Corsages, page 22. Give each daisy a button center, and as you sew the buttons on, leave threads hanging at the back for fastening onto the chandelier.

Tea light holders Using the template on page 138 and following the instructions for 3-d Seamless Objects, page 124, make all five simultaneously from two layers of felt, remembering they will shrink by about 20% and that they will need to fit the battery-powered tea lights. Allow for about 1 oz (25 g) of citrus green, and ½ oz (15 g) each of the other colors used. Use citrus green for the inner layer; for the outer layer, make two candy pink with red stripes, two orange with rose pink stripes, and one bright red with candy stripes. After removing the plastic templates, cut the edges into a deep petal-like scallop, using pins to mark out if necessary. Using plenty of soap, shape the bases into cup shapes from the inside, and felt the newly cut edges. Remove all traces of soap and give a final roll to finish. Re-shape into little cups whilst still damp and stuff with old wool to dry.

MAKING THE FRAME

1. To make the base ring use the 12-gauge (2 mm) wire to form a circle about 12–15½ in. (30–40 cm) in diameter, coiling the wire around three times for strength. Secure in six places using small cut lengths of the 18-gauge (0.9 mm) wire, bending round and twisting with the pliers (**A**). Trim and tuck the excess ends to make them safe. Make the smaller top ring measuring about 6–8 in. (15–20 cm) in diameter.

2. To make the top hanging piece, cut three 10 in. (25 cm) lengths from the 18-gauge (0.9 mm) wire. Measure and mark three equidistant points on the smaller top ring and coil the newly cut wire pieces around securely, trimming and tucking the attached ends. Run your finger along the wire lengths to curl them in slightly. Use some beading wire to attach the three lengths together at the top, using the pliers to form decorative loops at the ends (**B**). Secure in a couple of places with beading wire and add a final loop for hanging.

3. To make the top three hanging arms, cut three 13¾ in. (35 cm) lengths of 18-gauge (0.9mm) wire. One at a time, fold each in half and make a small loop at the folded end by twisting to hang the larger needle felted balls from later. Using the pliers and extra bits of beading wire if necessary, attach the other end to the top ring at the same three points marked out in step 2, but this time point the arms over and down by curling them round slightly.

4. It is now time to join together the smaller top ring and the larger base ring and make the tea light arms in one fell swoop! Cut five 23½ in. (60 cm) lengths of 18-gauge (0.9 mm) wire. Mark five equidistant points around both the top ring and the base ring. For ease of access, you will find it best to hang up the constructed top part before continuing.

5. Using the pliers wrap ¾–1⅛ in. (2–3 cm) of the cut lengths of wire around the top ring at the marked points until fastened securely. Working wire by wire, measure about 15¾ in. (40 cm) down the length and wrap a few times around a marked point on the base ring, leaving a spare 8 in. (20 cm) of wire at the end. Fold the remaining 8 in. (20 cm) in half, and as you double back form a loop. Secure the end around the base ring again. These are the protruding arms for the tea light holders and chandelier drops (**C**).

6. Now that the basic frame is made, start to wrap the wires with the variegated wool. Before you start, wind the wool into several smaller balls, as this will make it easier. Cover up as much of the wire as you can by winding the wool round and round each piece of wire, or leave bits showing if desired (**D**)!

ASSEMBLING THE CHANDELIER

Note refer to the photo on page 58 for a guide to the positioning of the felt components.

1. Keeping three large felt beads back for the top hanging arms, and using a very large sharp needle or bodkin, thread a selection of beads and medium-sized felt balls onto each felt strand, adding large plastic and glass beads here and there if you are using them (I used plastic flower-shaped and round flat glass beads). You will have to force the felt strands through the balls and beads quite hard and it is helpful to use the pliers to pull the needle through. If you find that this is too difficult, you can sew the beads and balls onto the strands using matching thread.

Attach them quite randomly, allowing for a few on each strand, choosing colors that contrast well.

2. Tie all the felt strands onto the top ring, alternating colors so they contrast well. Supplement any obviously large gaps using further lengths of the variegated yarn.

3. Next attach the double daisies around the top ring using the threads left at the back of the flowers. Tie each one on securely, alternating and contrasting colors.

4. Drape the felt strands over the base ring and bunch together at the bottom. Secure with a felt strand and tie on a couple of roses as a finishing touch.

5. Add the remaining roses around the base ring, tying on each with the threads left at the back and spacing them out evenly.

6. Add the smaller single daisies about 2 in. (5 cm) beneath the roses, at the point the strands start to go inward. Tie each one on as before.

7. Insert each battery-powered tea light into its felted holder (this is easier to do before you attach them), and then sew the base of each holder in place in and around the protruding wire loop. Thread three small felt balls onto some cotton or yarn and hang each chandelier drop beneath them. Attach to the base of each tea light holder using small stitches in a matching thread.

8. Thread some yarn through a large felt bead and then through one of the large daisy balls. Tie onto each of the loops at the end of the top three hanging arms.

9. Thread some yarn through the remaining large spotty ball and tie it onto one of the hanging strands at the very bottom of the chandelier.

10. As a final touch, you can dot some feather butterflies here and there as desired.

MAKING THE FRAME

A.

B.

C.

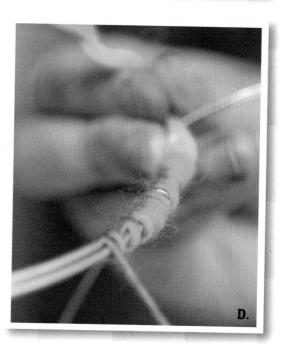

D.

USEFUL THINGS
FOR YOUR HOME

HOMELY HARMONY PINBOARD

◆◆◆◆◆◆◆◆◆◆◆◆◆◆◆◆◆◆◆◆◆◆◆◆◆◆

Let this pretty pinboard keep things spic-and-span around your home by storing everything in its place! There's a giant pocket at the bottom for odds and ends, and a large area at the top for pinning up important things.

MATERIALS

◆◆◆◆◆◆◆◆◆◆◆◆◆◆◆◆◆◆◆

MERINO WOOL TOPS

For the background square
3 oz (75 g) of pale blue
2 oz (50 g) of peppermint green
½ oz (15 g) of pale turquoise
Small amounts of gold, bright yellow,
bright red, cherry red, candy pink, and black

For the pocket
3 oz (75 g) each of white, sage green, and salmon pink
Small amounts of white, rose pink, gold, candy pink,
dark olive, grass green, red, and pale pink

> **TECHNIQUES**
> SIMPLE FLAT FELT
> (PAGE 120),
> NEEDLE FELTING
> (PAGE 134),
> 3-D SEAMLESS OBJECTS
> (PAGE 124),
> MAKING A HANDLE/
> STRAND
> (PAGE 130)

For the scalloped edge to background square
2 oz (50 g) of salmon pink
1 oz (25 g) of peach
Small amounts of rose pink, candy pink,
custard yellow, and pale pink

For the scalloped edge to pocket
1oz (25 g) of lilac
Small amounts of dusty mauve

For the flowers
1 oz (25 g) of salmon pink
½ oz (15 g) each of peach, candy pink, pale pink,
white, and cherry red
Small amounts of custard yellow, gold, rose pink,
pale pink, bright yellow, and black

For the stems and leaves
½ oz (15 g) each of dark olive, jade, sage green,
grass green, and cherry red

For the bird
1 oz (25 g) of bright red
Small amounts of pale pink, white,
candy pink, turquoise, and black

OTHER REQUIREMENTS
Wet felting essentials (see page 116)
36- and 38-gauge felting needles and foam
Cork pinboard of your choice
18-gauge (0.9 mm) galvanized wire
Fine-nosed pliers
Strong fabric glue
Pink variegated yarn

Finished size: 24 x 24 in. (61 x 61 cm)

METHOD

MAKING THE BACKGROUND SQUARE

1. To make the flat felt, start by measuring the size of the board minus the frame. Add 20% to your measurements to allow for shrinkage and mark out this area onto a waterproof surface.

2. Start laying out the pale blue onto the marked area with the fibers all facing in the same direction. Add a finer layer of peppermint green over the top in the other direction. Add lots of small wispy circles of pale turquoise over the top.

3. Cover, wet, soap and rub on this side for about 20 minutes, then turn and repeat the rubbing on the reverse.

4. Rinse briefly in warm water, then do a complete roll on both sides (see Simple Flat Felt, steps 12 and 13, page 123).

5. Rinse again in very hot then very cold water, and be sure to remove all traces of soap. Keep an eye on shrinkage as you rinse to make sure the piece ends up large enough to cover the board. Leave to dry.

6. Add needle felted details using a 38-gauge needle, referring to the instructions for Decorative Needle Felting on page 134. Using the photograph as a guide, use pins to mark out the scrolling gold frame. Use gold to needle in the rough shape, then add highlights of bright yellow. Add a small red circle at the end of each coil, with a smaller black dot in the center of each.

7. At the center top, needle on a large red heart between the coils, adding highlights of candy pink and cherry red. Repeat for the smaller hearts at each corner.

MAKING THE SCALLOPED EDGINGS

1. The scalloped edgings for the background square and the pocket are laid out and felted at the same time. Lay out an area of salmon pink measuring about 8 x 58½ in. (20 cm x 1.5 m), adding the scalloped edging shapes to both long edges. Make the scallops as even as you can by eye—but it doesn't matter if they are all slightly different. Using the wool quite wispily, add smaller amounts of rose pink, candy pink, peach, custard yellow, and pale pink on top, as highlights.

2. Alongside, lay out another smaller area about 24 in. (60 cm) long of lilac, adding a scalloped shape to one edge only; use the dusty mauve to highlight the scalloped edge.

3. Felt both of these scalloped edge pieces following steps 3, 4 and 5 for Making the Background Square.

4. When the felt is dry, cut off the scalloped edges about 2 in. (5 cm) deep from the pink piece. Pin these into place around the edge of the background square and sew together with blanket stitch, using a contrasting embroidery thread.

5. Cut the scalloped edge off the lilac piece and set aside.

MAKING THE GIANT POCKET

1. You have two choices here: you can either make a felt bag in the pocket shape around a plastic template and cut it in half (as I did), or you can make a piece of thickish flat felt, which is quicker and uses about 50% less wool. The advantages of making the felt bag is that you can keep the curved edge and base, which makes the pocket stronger and also looks nicer.

2. Using the template on page 137 (enlarged by 200%) and referring to 3-d Seamless Objects, page 124, lay out a layer of salmon pink wool horizontally, overlapping the edges of the template. Cover, wet, soap and rub for five minutes. Remove the netting, turn over and fold in the edges, and repeat on the other side to complete the inner layer.

3. Repeat step 2 using white for the middle layer and laying the wool in the opposite—vertical—direction.

4. For the first side of the outer layer, lay the sage green horizontally allowing for a larger than normal overlap. On top of this add fine white vertical stripes, and small flowers using wispy amounts of rose pink, candy pink, red, and orange, with a spot of gold in the center. Make little leaves from dark olive and grass green. Cover, wet, soap and rub for about 20–30 minutes, or until the fibers no longer move around and are well matted together.

(continues on page 70)

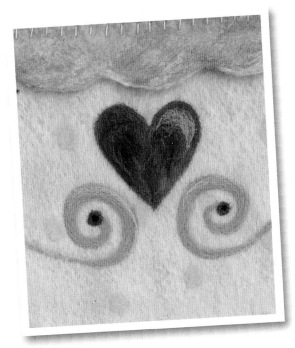

Start by needle felting a rough plan of your design with one color, then gradually add more details and colors to make the designs stand out from the background.

5. Turn again and fold in the edges, this time just filling in the center with the remaining green wool tops. (It is not necessary to add the pattern to this side as it will be cut away before attaching to the board.) Cover, wet, soap and rub for another 20–30 minutes or so.

6. Rinse briefly in warm water, then do a complete roll on both sides as described on page 127 (see 3-d Seamless Objects, step 9). Rinse again in hot water and roll again about 10 times.

7. Cut open the top edge with some small sharp scissors and remove the template. Felt the newly cut edges with a little water and soap. Finish by rinsing in very hot then very cold water, taking care to remove all traces of soap. Leave to dry.

8. Cut away the central area of the back of the pocket, leaving about 2–2¼ in. (5–6 cm) around the edge. On the front of the pocket, sew the lilac scalloped edge along the top using blanket stitch.

MAKING THE FLOWERS

1. Referring to the Rose and Daisy Corsages, page 22, make two daisies for the top corners—one pale pink and one white—and one from cherry red for the middle of the pocket. Add needle felting details (see photo opposite).

2. Referring to the Rose and Daisy Corsages, page 22, make a rose in colors to match the pink scalloped edges, and some leaves in dark olive and jade, adding on needle felted leaf veins.

3. To make the rosebuds, use the same colored felt as the main rose, and the templates on pages 137 and 139. Cut the larger shape (A) first for the center and coil up. Needle together at the base to shape. Now cut a few of the smaller petals (B) and needle them on, one at a time, overlapping them slightly as you go. Cut a small circle of green felt, making a deep zigzag around the edge of it. Cut a small hole in the center for threading through stems (see step 4) and bring up the sepals around each rosebud. Needle felt everything together, and add a little glue too for permanence.

4. To make the flower stems, felt some strands (see Making a Handle/Strand, page 130) and attach these to the flowers using the felting needle and/or glue.

Although it seems like slightly more work, making a 3-d bag for the pocket (as opposed to just a flat piece of felt) will allow you to keep the rounded edges, making the pocket stronger and more substantial.

MAKING THE BIRD

1. The pinboard bird is made in the same way as the Lesser Spotted Felty Warbler (see page 54), although it is a little smaller. Make the body using red wool.

2. Needle felt spots onto the bird's back using white wool, and make the beak using pale pink. Add a candy pink eye, with a turquoise outline and a black center.

3. Wrap the wire legs in a pink variegated yarn.

ASSEMBLING THE PINBOARD

1. First attach the background square to your cork pinboard. The best way is to sew it on using a strong thread and small running stitches. This will be more permanent than glue and avoids visible glue marks.

2. Arrange the flowers at the top corners and sew in place.

3. Apply glue to the back edge of the pocket and fix in place; then add small stitches too from behind. The pocket will need to be very securely fixed if you are going to put heavy things in it, so don't leave any gaps!

4. Sew and glue the red flower onto the center of the top edge.

5. The little bird can perch anywhere you choose and can be attached using small stitches from behind. Alternatively you could glue his feet to the top of the board.

The daisy centers are needle felted in gold and bright yellow, and a few black dots have been added to the largest white daisy.

TOTALLY TROPICAL KNITTING NEEDLE ROLL

◆◆◆◆◆◆◆◆◆◆◆◆◆◆◆◆◆◆◆◆◆◆◆◆◆

Felt, quilt and sew this magnificent knitting needle storage case and wow the crowd at your local knitting group! Choose a colorful cotton lining to complement the tropical felted design. Roomy internal pockets have space for all your needles, yet it rolls up neatly and is held together with matching fabric ties. Adapt the size to make it as big as you like!

TECHNIQUES
SIMPLE FLAT FELT
(PAGE 120)

MATERIALS

◆◆◆◆◆◆◆◆◆◆◆◆◆◆◆◆◆◆◆

MERINO WOOL TOPS
1½ oz (40 g) each of bright olive and bright yellow
Small amounts of gold, orange, red, candy pink,
salmon pink, light turquoise, turquoise, cerise,
kingfisher blue, lilac, delphinium, and grass green

OTHER REQUIREMENTS
Wet felting essentials (see page 116)
20 in. (0.5 m) cotton fabric
20 in. (0.5 m) batting (wadding)

Finished size: approximately 15 x 12 in. (38 x 31 cm)

NOTES
For my lining fabric I chose Kaffe Fassett's Paisley Jungle in lime.
For this needle roll I used half a yard/meter, but if you make a
larger case, you may need more.

METHOD

LAYING OUT THE WOOL TOPS

1. Mark out an area 15¾ x 25½ in. (40 x 65 cm). Remember the finished felt will shrink by about 20%, so if you want to make your piece larger (or smaller) adjust accordingly at this point.

2. Lay out the bright olive wool over the marked area with all fibers facing in one direction; then lay the bright yellow over the top with all the fibers facing the opposite way.

3. Next create the candy pink ferns by laying out three large leaves with red highlights under each frond. In between these, create a few large pale turquoise circles with lilac, delphinium and grass green swirls around the outside. Dot orange circles within, each with a red center, and add a salmon pink circle in the middle, also with a red center.

4. Now add some small orange circles onto the bright yellow background, and also some small cerise circles with turquoise and kingfisher blue centers.

5. Lastly, lay a little bright olive up the spine of each fern, with cerise at the base of the stem.

6. Cover with netting, wet down, soap up, adjust, and rub the wool for about 20–30 minutes until the fibers feel joined together.

7. Briefly rinse in warm water, then do a complete roll on both sides (see Simple Flat Felt, steps 12 and 13, page 123). Rinse under very hot water, then freezing cold water, removing all traces of soap, and do another complete roll again. Leave to dry.

QUILTING THE FELT

Note this stage is optional and you could omit if you choose to.

1. Cut a piece of batting about the same size as the finished felted piece. Pin the batting to the wrong side of the felt.

2. Using matching thread, hand or machine sew around the large and small circles.

3. Cut the edges of the batting away if there is any excess hanging over the sides.

Candy pink ferns and multicolored dots and spots contrast well with the vibrant yellow background for this totally tropical felting.

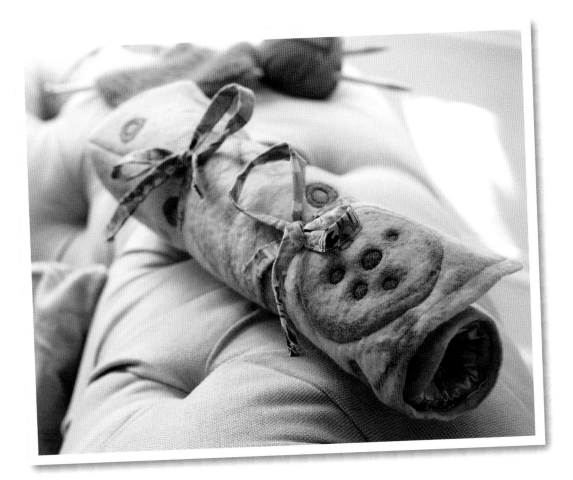

MAKING UP THE NEEDLE ROLL

1. Cut a piece of matching cotton lining fabric slightly larger than the felt and turn the edges under all the way around; pin together so the fabric is just hidden on top of the batting inside.

2. Sew all the way around the edge. Now fold up the bottom edge of the felt and lining by about 4¼ in. (11 cm) and sew along each side. Now add two more lines of sewing to create the pockets for the knitting needles to "sit" in.

3. Finally cut two strips of leftover fabric about 1⅛ x 25½ in. (3 x 65 cm). Working on one piece at a time, iron in the raw edges and the ends, and fold in half to create a long ribbon tie. Sew a seam all the way down and iron flat again.

4. Attach each ribbon tie to the outside of the felt along one side at equal intervals. Fill the pockets with your knitting needles, roll up and neatly tie the ribbons to keep everything in place.

Before the case is lined and pieced together, the felt is machine quilted with batting, to make it more protective.

CANDY-COATED CUPCAKE TEA COZY

◆ ◆ ◆ ◆ ◆ ◆ ◆ ◆ ◆ ◆ ◆ ◆ ◆ ◆ ◆ ◆ ◆ ◆ ◆ ◆

Keep your teapot warm inside this candy-pink cupcake-shaped tea cozy, complete with sugar sprinkles. This is a two layer project, worked around a plastic template. Extra sprinkles have been needle felted onto the "icing" once the wet felting is complete for mouth-watering texture. The cherry on top can be incorporated into the template shape, or a small red felt ball can be added afterward.

MATERIALS

◆ ◆ ◆ ◆ ◆ ◆ ◆ ◆ ◆ ◆ ◆ ◆ ◆ ◆ ◆ ◆

MERINO WOOL TOPS

3 oz (75 g) of lilac
1½ oz (40 g) each of candy pink and sage green
½ oz (15 g) each of pale pink and salmon pink
Small amounts of dark olive, pale turquoise,
rose pink, red, citrus, and lots of tiny dots
of different colors for the felted sprinkles

OTHER REQUIREMENTS

Wet felting essentials (see page 116)
Strong template plastic
38-gauge felting needle and foam
Small amount of Angelina glitter fiber

Finished size: 10 x 13 in. (27 x 35 cm) excluding cherry

*TECHNIQUES
3-D SEAMLESS OBJECTS
(PAGE 124),
NEEDLE FELTING
(PAGE 134)*

METHOD

WET FELTING THE TEA COZY SHAPE

1. Using the template on page 138, enlarge by 300%, or to at least 20% bigger than you intend your final tea cozy to be to allow for shrinkage. Cut out the cupcake shape from strong template plastic.

2. Lay out a layer of lilac wool vertically, overlapping the edges of the template. Cover with netting, wet, soap and rub for a few minutes. Turn the template over and fold in the edges. Repeat on the other side.

3. For the top layer and laying the wool out horizontally, lay out candy pink at the top to about halfway down, and sage green for the bottom half, allowing for an overlap. To make the cupcake case, add vertical stripes onto the sage green using small amounts of dark olive, pale turquoise, and citrus green.

4. Now add the different colored icing on top of the candy pink cake, graduating down from pale pink at the very top through to salmon pink at the bottom. Place a small amount of Angelina glitter fiber on top (I used the Aurora Borealis colorway) and trap it in by overlaying with some very wispy pink wool fibers.

5. Define the bottom edge of the icing by adding a stripe of rose pink, and then add tiny dots of different colors for the sprinkles!

6. Cover, wet, soap and rub for about 20–30 minutes, or until all the fibers are securely attached together. Turn over and fold in the edges.

7. You are now working on the final side. Repeat steps 2–4 to fill in the center section, and remembering that no overlap is required this time. Cover, wet, soap and rub for a further 30 minutes. Make sure all the fibers are well felted together.

8. Briefly rinse in warm water, then do a complete roll on both sides (see 3-d Seamless Objects, step 9, page 124). Rinse under very hot water, then roll briefly again.

9. Carefully cut open along the base and remove the template. Soap, rub and felt the newly cut edges.

10. Rinse again using very hot then very cold water, making sure all traces of soap are removed. Roll again until you are happy with the shrinkage. Leave to dry.

Once the tea cozy is made, add further texture and interest by needle felting small balls of wool tops onto the finished felt.

NEEDLE FELTING THE "ICING"

1. Place a foam pad inside the tea cozy under the area you will be working on. You will need very small amounts of lots of different color wools to create the best effect. Using slightly more wool than you would normally when needle felting, roll between your fingers into a small ball. Start to needle the woolly blob onto the base of the icing area, mainly stabbing around its edges, so that the wool forms a little bump.

2. As you add more and more different colors, you can achieve a raised bumpy 3-d effect, which adds depth and texture to the tea cozy. Keep stabbing and adding color around and in between the bumps, rather than stabbing the centers of them. It's a matter of personal preference how much you add, and you can keep going until the cake looks heavy with icing!

The raised needle felting makes it look as if the cupcake tea cozy is covered with real icing!

VARIEGATED VINTAGE PLANT BASKETS

◆◆◆◆◆◆◆◆◆◆◆◆◆◆◆◆◆◆◆◆◆◆◆◆◆◆

Envelop old plant pots in new felt robes with these vintage-style plant baskets. Made to stand with round bases, they can accommodate the most verdant of foliage! Made in two different colorways, each adorned with a felt rose, I have added a handle to one, which gives a nice finishing touch, especially for a gift. This is a two layer project worked around a plastic template.

TECHNIQUES
3-D SEAMLESS OBJECTS (PAGE 124),
MAKING A HANDLE STRAND (PAGE 130)

MATERIALS

◆◆◆◆◆◆◆◆◆◆◆◆◆◆◆◆◆

MERINO WOOL TOPS

For the pink basket

2 oz (50 g) each of white and pale pink
1 oz (25 g) each of candy pink and rose pink
1 oz (25 g) of pale pink for the handle
Small amounts of red, candy pink, grass green, and gold

For the blue/beige basket

2 oz (50 g) of white
Small amounts of sage green, black, chocolate brown, pale turquoise,
kingfisher, royal blue, peppermint green, and mid olive
Also 2 oz (50 g) of oatmeal Blue Faced Leicester
Small amounts of wool nepps and silk tops

OTHER REQUIREMENTS

Wet felting essentials (see page 116)
Strong template plastic
Felt roses
Embroidery thread

Finished size: height 6 in. (14 cm); diameter 6 in. (14 cm)

METHOD

WET FELTING THE PINK PLANT BASKET

1. Using the template on page 136, enlarge by 200%, or to at least 20% bigger than you intend your final plant pot to be to allow for shrinkage. Cut out the plant basket shape from strong template plastic.
2. Lay out a layer of white wool vertically, overlapping the edges of the template. Cover with netting, wet, soap and rub for a few minutes. Turn the template over and fold in the edges. Repeat on the other side.
3. For the top layer, lay out the pale pink in the opposite direction allowing for a generous overlap. Add wispy red circles randomly on top of the pink background layer, each with a circle of candy pink inside and a small gold center. Form some leaf shapes from the grass green wool and make two wispy green leaves for each "flower" circle.
4. Cover, wet, soap and rub for about 20–30 minutes or until all the fibers are securely attached together. Turn over and fold in the edges.

5. You are now working on the final side. Repeat steps 3–4 to fill in the center section, remembering that no overlap is required this time. Cover, wet, soap and rub for a further 30 minutes. Make sure all the fibers are well felted together.
6. Briefly rinse in warm water, then do a complete roll on both sides (see 3-d Seamless Objects, step 9, page 127). Rinse under very hot water, then roll briefly again.
7. Carefully cut open along the top of the plant basket and remove the template. Now place about seven pins at an equal distance apart around the top edge as a guide to cutting the scalloped petal edge. Using very sharp small scissors, make a slit at each pin, and then round off the sides of each "petal". You can choose to rub and felt the newly cut edges, or leave them for now to blanket stitch later.

FORMING THE PLANT BASKET BASE

1. Make the felt quite wet and very soapy, and place it on a table. Rubbing from the inside, start to form a base, using the soap to help shape and sculpt. Keep working it until it is round in shape and then manipulate a rim from the outside.
2. Rinse again using very hot then very cold water, making sure all traces of soap are removed. Roll again until you are happy with the shrinkage, then re-shape and leave to dry.

MAKING THE HANDLE AND FINISHING THE BASKET

1. Referring to Making a Handle/Strand, page 130, make a handle from pale pink wool tops; sew on.
2. Trim the handle with a rose made using a combination of orange and candy pink, with citrus and grass green leaves (see Rose and Daisy Corsages, page 22, for instruction).
3. Finish the scalloped edging with a large blanket stitch using red embroidery thread.

TIP
To protect the felt plant basket, sit the inner plant pot in a strong plastic bag.

MAKING THE BLUE PLANT BASKET

Follow Wet Felting the Pink Plant Basket, steps 1 and 2. For the top layer, lay out the oatmeal Blue Faced Leicester wool tops in the opposite direction allowing for a generous overlap and adding small wisps of all the other colors quite randomly over the top. Add a few wool nepps and some silk tops for textural interest, and put small cobwebby amounts of wool on top of them to keep them in place. Continue as for the pink plant basket, but omit the cutting of the flower petals. Form the plant basket base and leave to dry. Finish with a pale turquoise blanket stitch around the rim at the base of the basket, and trim the front with a rose, made using candy pink and orange, with leaves in bright olive.

EGGY PEGGY CLOTHESPIN BAG

Make washday fun with this cute little egg-shaped bag to hang on the line.
Using springtime colors and based around a plastic template, the shape is cut on the side
to make the opening. This bag is made using two layers of wool.

MATERIALS

MERINO WOOL TOPS
2⅓ oz (60 g) of mid olive
1 oz (25 g) each of pale yellow olive and eau de nil
⅔ oz (20 g) of pale pink
½ oz (15 g) of cherry red

OTHER REQUIREMENTS
Wet felting essentials (see page 116)
Strong template plastic
Strong fabric glue
Ribbon for hanging

Finished size: 10 x 8 in. (25 x 20 cm)

TECHNIQUES
3-D SEAMLESS OBJECTS
(PAGE 124),
MAKING A BALL
(PAGE 133)

NOTES
The clothespin bag is made just like a normal felt bag, but when
you come to cut it open—instead of slicing around the top as
usual—you will make a small insertion in the front top half of the
bag and gradually cut this into an opening, through which you will
remove the template. Make the hole large enough to get your hand
in and out and high enough so your clothespins don't fall out!

METHOD

WET FELTING THE BAG SHAPE

1. Using the template on page 139, enlarge by 300%, remembering that the finished item will shrink by about 20%.

2. Lay out a layer of mid olive wool vertically, overlapping the edges of the template. Cover with netting, wet, soap and rub for a few minutes. Turn the template over and fold in the edges. Repeat on the other side.

3. For the top layer, lay out the pale yellow olive and eau de nil in alternating horizontal stripes about ¾ in. (2 cm) high allowing for a generous overlap.

4. Cover, wet, soap and rub for about 20–30 minutes or until all the fibers are securely attached together. Turn over and fold in the edges.

5. You are now working on the final side. Repeat steps 2–4 to fill in the center section, remembering that no overlap is required this time. Cover, wet, soap and rub for a further 30 minutes. Make sure all the fibers are well felted together.

6. Briefly rinse in warm water, then do a complete roll on both sides (see 3-d Seamless Objects, step 9, page 127). Rinse under very hot water, then roll briefly again.

7. Using small sharp scissors, start to cut the opening for the bag on one side toward the top of the bag. Don't make it too large. (You can pin it out first if you want to.) Remove the template and trim to neaten if necessary. Wet the edges down, add a little soap and rub for about five minutes until felted.

8. Rinse again using very hot then very cold water, making sure all traces of soap are removed. Roll again until you are happy with the shrinkage; re-shape and leave to dry.

EMBELLISHING THE BAG

1. Make a small square piece of flat felt using the pale pink wool tops (see Simple Flat Felt, page 120). Cut out seven small circles with a diameter of about 1 in. (2.5 cm) to make four-petal daisies (see Rose and Daisy Corsages, page 22).

2. Make four tiny felt balls (see Making a Ball, page 133); slice each in half and glue to the center of the pink flowers. When dry, sew and glue the flowers onto the bag using a matching thread.

3. Finally, attach the hanging ribbon at the top. Make a small hole with the end of a pair of scissors and poke the ends of the ribbon through. Simply tie a knot on the inside of the bag to secure.

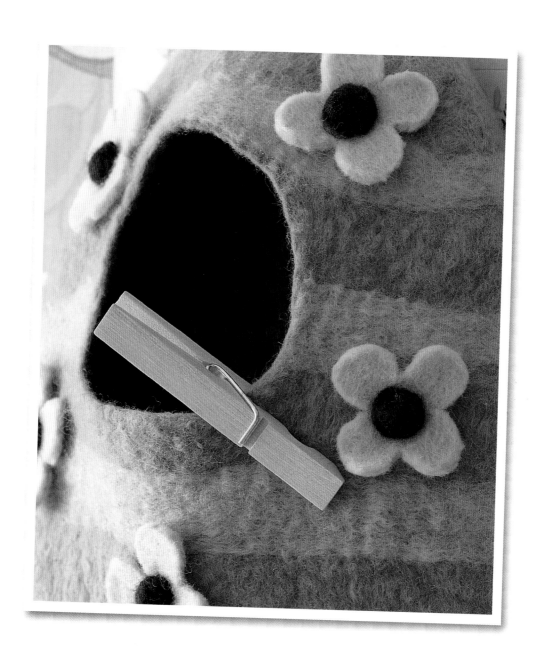

ALWAYS WORK WITH CHILDREN AND ANIMALS

COZY-GO-LIGHTLY TODDLER SLIPPERS

◆◆◆◆◆◆◆◆◆◆◆◆◆◆◆◆◆◆◆◆◆◆◆◆

When little feet must do the walking, these toddler slippers are just the ticket.
They are felted around polystyrene shoe lasts (forms), and you can choose to finish them in
one of two styles. The main instructions provided are for the Mary-Jane design—to make the
bootie follow the variations in the box on page 93. Make sure you attach a non-slip sole to the
base of the finished slippers.

MATERIALS

◆◆◆◆◆◆◆◆◆◆◆◆◆◆◆◆◆◆

MERINO WOOL TOPS

For the Mary-Janes

$1^1/_2$ oz (40 g) of lilac for the inner layer
$1^1/_2$ oz (40 g) of dusty pink for the middle layer
$1^1/_2$ oz (40 g) of dusty mauve for the outer layer
Small amounts of pale turquoise, pale yellow olive,
salmon pink, eau de nil, pale pink, sage green, and teal
Also small amounts of oatmeal Blue Faced Leicester

For the booties

$1^1/_2$ oz (40 g) of cream for the inner layer
$1^1/_2$ oz (40 g) of cream for the middle layer
Small amounts of mid olive, chocolate brown,
cream, and eau de nil
Also $1^1/_2$ oz (40 g) of oatmeal Blue Faced Leicester for the outer layer

OTHER REQUIREMENTS

Wet felting essentials (see page 116)
Pair of polystyrene shoe lasts in the appropriate size
Two plastic bags big enough to cover the lasts
Two elastic bands
Strong fabric glue
Sheepskin insoles (optional)
Slipper soles (see notes overleaf)
Small amounts of wool nepps
Angelina glitter fibers
Pink linen thread, pretty elastic, four decorative buttons
and two roses for decorating the Mary-Janes
Giant dusty pink rickrack and two roses for decorating the booties

Finished size: length $5^1/_2$ in. (14 cm) (US size 6/7)

TECHNIQUES
USING A SHOE LAST
(PAGE 128)

METHOD

WET FELTING THE SLIPPERS

1. First prepare the shoe lasts (see Using a Shoe Last, step 1, page 128). Now prepare the wool tops: split each 1½ oz (40 g) length in half to give two equal lengths—one for each foot. Split each length again into three equal lengths, one for the sole, one for the left side of the slipper and one for the right side.

2. To make the Mary-Janes, and working on one foot at a time, use the lilac first to lay down and work the inner layer as described on pages 128–129 (see Using a Shoe Last, steps 2 and 3), covering the sole first then moving on to each side, making sure that the entire last is completely encased in wool—including the very top. Repeat for the other foot.

3. Using the dusty pink next, lay down and work the middle layer in the same way.

4. Using the dusty mauve lengths, lay and work the outer layer but before rubbing the two sides, add the details and designs first, decorating with a mixture of swirls and circles. Use wispy amounts of all the different colors randomly around the slippers. Add wool nepps and Angelina glitter fibers (I used the Calypso Blue colorway) into the design taking care to cover these areas with a little cobwebby wool so that they are held in place. When you are happy with the design, start rubbing—you will need to work at it this time for about 20 minutes on each foot or until all the designs and fibers have firmly matted together.

5. Remove the netting and spend a little more time rubbing both feet, using plenty of soap so you don't dislodge any of the designs. When you are totally confident that the designs have felted together well, put the slippers in a washing machine on a 140°F (60°C) wash cycle. Add a pair of old jeans (or similar) to the wash to facilitate the felting process.

TRIMMING AND FITTING THE SLIPPERS

1. Remove the lasts (see Using a Shoe Last, step 5, page 129) and trim the slippers carefully, using pins to mark out cutting lines and erring on the side of caution. Trim away the top of the slippers gradually, as you don't want to end up with too much missing, until the opening is sufficient to get the feet inside. Leave to dry.

2. Check the fit. If the slippers are a little roomy you could add some cozy sheepskin insoles. If they are really large, however, it is a good idea to shrink them a little under the tap. Take great care not to shrink them too much, as extremes of temperature will reduce them in size quite dramatically, especially if any soap remains. Remove all traces of soap if you add any more. Once the lasts have been removed, do not put them back in the washing machine as this will result in disaster!

FINISHING THE SLIPPERS

1. Sew a little decorative elastic across the slipper opening and add a button at each side (I used all different ones). Finish the cut edges with a decorative blanket stitch using a strong linen thread.

2. Trim each slipper with roses made using a combination of lilac and dusty mauve (see Rose and Daisy Corsages, page 22).

MAKING THE BOOTIES

The booties are wet felted in exactly the same way as the Mary-Janes, but use cream wool tops for both the inner and middle layers, and for the outer layer, lay a background of the oatmeal Blue Faced Leicester before adding the swirling pattern design. Again, give some texture and interest by adding a few wool nepps and some Angelina glitter fibers (I used the Peacock colorway this time). After felting and removing the booties from the lasts, just trim the very tops and make a small slit down the front, making sure the child's feet will get in and out easily. To finish, pin and sew the giant rickrack around the opening, and trim with roses made using a combination of pale pink and salmon pink.

PET PETALS
PET BED

◆◆◆◆◆◆◆◆◆◆◆◆◆◆◆◆◆◆◆◆◆◆◆◆◆

Make your doting doggie or curious cat their own version of a Chesterfield sofa
to luxuriate on with this pretty pet bed. The felt is made really thick, so it is substantial
and will stand up to wear and tear, and if the felt gets muddy, simply wait until dry
and brush off briskly!

TECHNIQUES
SIMPLE FLAT FELT
(PAGE 120)

MATERIALS

◆◆◆◆◆◆◆◆◆◆◆◆◆◆◆◆◆◆

MERINO WOOL TOPS
3 oz (75 g) each of pale yellow olive, red,
white, and grass green
2 oz (50 g) each of gold and cherry red
1 oz (25 g) of racing green
½ oz (15 g) each of rose pink, light turquoise, and black
Small amounts of candy pink and turquoise

OTHER REQUIREMENTS
Wet felting essentials (see page 116)
Cushion pad about 25½ in. (65 cm) in diameter (or stuffing)
Stuffing for petals
3¼ yd (3 m) batting (wadding)
3¼ yd (3 m) cotton fabric for backing
Strong linen thread (or similar) for finishing

Finished size: about 40 in. (1 m) in diameter

NOTES
The pet bed shown is suitable for a medium-sized dog like
a cocker spaniel; reduce quantities and measurements by about
one-third for a very small dog or cat, or increase by one-third for
a larger dog.

You could also make this project as a floor cushion for
the kids, or scale it down to make a smaller cushion
for the sofa.

The circle for the center panel is made from six layers of wool
tops to make it really thick and substantial.

METHOD

◆◆◆◆◆◆◆◆◆◆◆◆◆◆◆◆◆◆◆◆◆◆◆◆◆◆◆

WET FELTING THE CENTER PANEL

1. Lay out a circle of white wool measuring 35½ in. (90 cm) in diameter. Lay two more white layers with fibers facing in alternating directions for each. Using the grass green, add another few layers in the same way.

2. Now add the darker racing green around the edge in a radial fashion, with the wispy ends facing inward, so the colors fade through a little.

3. Place wispy pale turquoise spots, accented with a little turquoise, randomly across the top. Make sure these aren't too thick otherwise it will be difficult to rub them together.

4. Finish by alternating small black and white circles around the edge.

5. Cover, wet, soap and rub together (see Simple Flat Felt, page 120, paying particular attention to step 9, Precision Wet Felting, page 123).

6. Roll and rinse until the felt has shrunk by about 20%. Leave to dry.

QUILTING AND BACKING THE CENTER PANEL

1. Cut a circle of batting the same size as the finished felt circle and pin together.

2. Quilt around the small turquoise spots. You can do so either by using a sewing machine with a free foot attachment, or by hand.

3. Cut a circle of backing fabric slightly larger than the felt circle. With wrong sides together, fold in the edges of the backing fabric until they are hidden just behind the finished edge of the felt circle. Pin and baste.

4. Leaving a gap so that you can insert the cushion pad or stuffing, sew together either by hand or machine, following the inside edge of the black and white design on the front, so that the black and white border stands free.

5. Insert the cushion pad (or stuffing), then finish the seam.

WET FELTING THE OUTER "PETAL" PANELS

Note working in the same way, make three of each color.

1. For the gold petals, lay out the soft yellow olive wool roughly 11 x 25½ in. (28 x 65 cm). Round the top into a petal shape. Build up at least three layers of wool and then add the gold wool around the edges to add lowlights that fade in.

2. Place a few wispy cherry red and rose pink spots randomly on top, and accent each with a little candy pink or bright red. Felt, quilt and sew as for the center panel, stuffing with some old wool tops (or similar).

3. Repeat for the red petals, using red as the base color with cherry red as the darker color for the lowlights on top, and adding spots in pale yellow olive and gold.

PIECING THE BED TOGETHER

1. Find a large work surface. Pin together all of the pieces, with the large circle in the center and the six petals slightly overlapping around the edges.

2. Using a really strong thread—such as linen thread—in matching colors, stitch all the pieces together from front to back, concealing the stitches where possible, and keeping the finished felt edges showing all the way around.

I love the "finished" edges of the handmade felt, so I have found a way of piecing the bed so you can see them all!

◆◆◆◆◆◆◆◆◆◆◆◆◆◆◆◆◆

JOLLY JESTER
CHRISTMAS STOCKING

◆◆◆◆◆◆◆◆◆◆◆◆◆◆◆◆◆◆◆◆◆◆

Imagine this colorful stocking stuffed full of presents hanging on the fireplace.
It is made entirely from recycled sweaters that have been felted in the washing machine. You
can really have fun cutting them up and putting them back together again for a new purpose.

MATERIALS

◆◆◆◆◆◆◆◆◆◆◆◆◆◆◆◆◆◆

Several recycled sweaters (see notes)
Seven small bells
Contrasting yarn/embroidery threads for decorative stitching
Ribbon for hanging

Finished size: 22 x 11½ in. (56 x 29 cm) at stocking top

NOTES

To make a multicolored stocking like mine,
you will need to use five or six different sweaters.

To make a one-color stocking, I would recommend
one large sweater or two small ones as a minimum.

Make sure the sweaters you choose have a high wool content
and that they are not made from superwash wool.
Sweaters labeled "hand-wash only" or "100% pure new wool"
are ideal as this suggests they will felt nicely.

Wash the sweaters at about 140°F (60°C); when you cut
them up they will not unravel or fray.

Alternatively, if you choose to, you could make the stocking
from pieces of ready-made colored wool felt.

METHOD

CUTTING THE COMPONENT PARTS OF THE STOCKING

Note refer to the templates on page 138–139 when cutting the main stocking shape and the heel and toe.

1. Start by cutting the main body about 22 in. (56 cm) high from the first sweater.

2. Cut the main foot shape about 12½ in. (32 cm) wide from a second sweater. Then cut the heel and toe, and also the top zigzag decoration from a third sweater.

3. The second layer of zigzag decoration is cut from a fourth sweater, and made slightly deeper so it hangs down underneath the other.

4. The circles have also been cut from felted sweaters, but you could just as easily use pieces of ready-made felt for this.

PIECING AND SEWING THE STOCKING PIECES

1. Pin, baste and sew the main body, foot, heel and toe together. I chose to sew mine by machine with the outer seams showing for a slightly rustic look.

2. Pin and baste the zigzag pieces around the stocking top and machine sew together.

TIP

Add texture and interest to your stocking by choosing and using sweaters in as many different colors and patterns as you can.

DECORATING AND FINISHING

1. Sew a contrasting blanket stitch around the top of the stocking by hand and accentuate the foot with a running stitch in the same color. Be careful not to sew through to the other side when stitching across the "ankle" or you will not be able to fill the foot with even more presents!

2. Cut about 13 red circles and 13 slightly smaller pink circles. Place a pink circle on top of a red circle and sew in place on the front of the stocking with a decorative star-shaped stitch. Oversew the edges of the red circles to hold them in place.

3. Finally, sew a small bell at the pointed ends of the top zigzag border and a small loop of ribbon to one side for hanging.

ROCKINGLY RETRO PET COLLAR

◆◆◆◆◆◆◆◆◆◆◆◆◆◆◆◆◆◆◆◆◆◆◆◆◆

Adorn your best furry friend with a suitably fluffy collar to match their personality.
Choose from two colorways, red and pink or blue and gold.
You will need to know how to crochet for this project, but only chain and single crochet
are used so it's nice and easy. The collar is felted in the washing machine, then cut to shape
and sewn. You can even add some bling to really show it off!

MATERIALS

◆◆◆◆◆◆◆◆◆◆◆◆◆◆◆◆◆

WASH & FILZ IT WOOL
Anchor 2 oz (50 g) 100% wool
Approximately 50 yd

For the red/pink collar
Color A = 2 oz (50 g) of red color 019
Color B = 2 oz (50 g) of pale pink color 010

For the blue/gold collar
Color A = 2 oz (50 g) of blue color 023
Color B = 2 oz (50 g) of gold color 024

OTHER REQUIREMENTS
US L-11 (8 mm) crochet hook
Stick on gems (optional)
Strong fabric glue
Buckle
D ring (optional)
Small length of narrow ribbon

Finished size: about ¾ x 11 in. (2 x 28 cm)

METHOD

CROCHETING THE COLLAR

1. Using color A, chain eight. Single crochet into the second chain from the hook and back along the row. Repeat another three rows in red. Change to color B and repeat another four rows.

2. Keep repeating and alternating colors A and B until the crocheted strip measures approximately 13 in. (33 cm) for a cat or a small/medium dog and about 15½ in. (40 cm) for a larger dog. Trim yarn ends neatly and make sure they are secure.

FELTING AND FINISHING

1. Wash the crocheted collar in your washing machine with a full load at 100°F (40°C) using detergent as normal.

2. Once felted, use large sharp scissors to trim and remove the sides. Use a center strip to get straight edges. Trim to size to fit the buckle. Sew the end into place around the D ring and then the buckle. If you're not using a D ring, make a small loop with the ribbon around the buckle end of the collar and sew in place.

3. Add gems with dabs of glue along the length of the collar if desired.

It's quick and easy to create many different collars from one piece of felted crochet. Once cut, they will not fray, and they can be embellished with gems.

TIP
To make a collar for a bigger dog, simply make your piece of crochet about 20% larger.

❖❖❖❖❖❖❖❖❖❖❖❖❖❖❖❖❖❖

BETTY CONFETTI FLOWER FAIRY

◆◆◆◆◆◆◆◆◆◆◆◆◆◆◆◆◆◆◆◆◆◆◆◆◆◆◆◆

This amazing fairy has a needle felted head and body joined together with wool-wrapped arms and neck. Her delicate dress is made in two parts—a nuno felted jacket formed around a template and a skirt made from individual felt "petals" sewn onto an underskirt. For her hair, kid mohair locks have been needle felted onto her head. She is a perfect little work of art more suitable as an ornament or keepsake rather than a toy.

MATERIALS

◆◆◆◆◆◆◆◆◆◆◆◆◆◆◆◆◆◆◆◆◆◆

TECHNIQUES
NEEDLE FELTING
(PAGE 134),
3-D SEAMLESS OBJECTS
(PAGE 124),
SIMPLE FLAT FELT
(PAGE 120)

MERINO WOOL TOPS
3 oz (75 g) of salmon pink for the body and head
½ oz (15 g) each of dusty mauve and
sage green for the petals
½ oz (15 g) of sage green for the underskirt
Small amounts of dusty pink, eau de nil, dark olive, and
pale yellow olive for the underskirt
Small amounts of black and red for the face

OTHER REQUIREMENTS
Wet felting essentials (see page 116)
36 and 38-gauge felting needles and multi-needle tool
29½ in. (75 cm) 18-gauge (0.9mm) galvanized wire and fine-nosed pliers
Knitting yarn to cover the arms and neck (see notes)
Strong fabric glue
Strong template plastic
Small button or buckle
About 8 in. (20 cm) square chiffon (or similar) for the jacket
Kid mohair locks and Angelina glitter fibers for the hair
Guinea-fowl feathers for the wings
Small bits of felt for the hair garland flowers

Finished size: 12 x 11 in. (30 x 28 cm)

NOTES
The slightly variegated knitting yarn used to wrap around Betty's
arms and neck was Colinette One Zero in Peaches and Cream.

METHOD

SCULPTING THE HEAD AND BODY

1. To make the head, take a tightly bunched ball of salmon pink and, using a multi-needle tool with 38-gauge needles, needle it until it forms a head shape measuring approximately 2½ in (6.5 cm). Shape it flatter on the front and back. Add facial details using a single 38-gauge needle, using very small amounts of black for the eyes and red for the heart-shaped mouth.

2. The body shape is approximately 8 in. (20 cm) in length, which tapers inward toward the top of the body and is shaped into a waist and skirt scallops at the base of the body (see Sculptural Needle Felting, page 135). Start by teasing the salmon wool apart a little, and push and roll it together to form a large blob that is slightly triangular and smaller at one end. Keep needling and refining it, adding more wool to it as you go, to make sure it is solid. It takes quite a while to get the shape right and it is often easier to "sculpt" using the slightly larger 38-gauge needles in the multi-needle tool.

3. To make the waist, stab with just one needle around the shape until a channel is formed in the wool. Likewise, scallop the skirt slightly by using the multi-needle tool or a single needle to indent (see photo); add more pieces of pink wool onto some areas and stab some areas in so they recede. Keep refining until you are happy with the shape.

MAKING THE NECK AND ARMS

1. Take the length of wire and fold in each end by about 6 in. (15 cm) to make the arms. To make the neck, twist together about 3 in. (8 cm) in the center using the pliers to point upward (see photo).

2. Start to wind the yarn around the arms and neck, but leave a small amount of wire sticking out at the top. Twist together tightly. Make a hole in the base of the head using a felting needle. Insert strong fabric glue into the hole, and then insert the twisted wire and leave to dry.

3. Place the head and wire arms onto the body and sew in place with the lightweight yarn, sewing round the arms through into the pink wool body to secure.

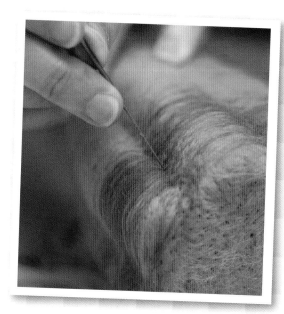

Using a single felting needle to refine the shape of Betty's body.

Making the arms and neck from wire.

NUNO FELTING THE JACKET

1. Use the template on page 137 to cut a template shape from strong template plastic for the top of Betty's dress. Lay some pieces of chiffon—or a similarly gauzy fabric—over the top of the template, overlapping the edges slightly. Cover with very small amounts of wispy wool in pale yellow olive, sage green and eau de nil. Cover with netting, wet down and soap up. Rub for about 5–10 minutes, then turn over, fold in the edges and add more chiffon on the back to meet the turned in edges. Cover with more wool to match the felt and repeat the wetting, soaping and rubbing.

2. When the fibers feel attached and matted, rinse and roll (see 3-d Seamless Objects, step 9, page 124). Cut open the base of the jacket, and remove the template. Make small slits at the ends of the sleeves and flare out for the cuffs. Repeat the rinsing and rolling, removing all traces of soap in the process.

3. Cut the jacket clean in half—this seems a little dramatic, but it's the only way you're going to get it on her! Put each of Betty's arms through the sleeves and sew up the back again with some small neat stitches in a matching thread. To fasten her jacket together in the front, use a small piece of yarn, fabric or felt and a matching buckle or button, and secure in place with glue and/or stitches.

WET FELTING THE PETAL SKIRT

1. The skirt is made in several sections to create the petal-like effect. The wool is laid out directly onto a waterproof surface. First use sage green to lay out about 20 heart shapes, each measuring about 4 in. (10 cm) wide. Add dusty mauve on top and highlight with eau de nil, pale yellow olive and dusty pink.

2. To make the sepal-like top of the skirt, lay out a series of conjoined leaves using the sage green, with some dark olive at the top and a highlight of dusty pink down the center of each leaf, using the template on page 137.

3. Felt the hearts and the sepals following the instructions for Simple Flat Felt, page 120, and leave to dry.

4. Make the underskirt from a spare piece of fabric or felt. Cut a circle about 6¼ in. (16 cm) in diameter. Cut away about a fifth of the circle, so that when the edges are brought together it is slightly cone shaped, checking that it will fit around Betty's waist.

5. Sew the finished hearts onto the skirt upside down, so that they overlap one another and hide the fabric underneath. Attach the sepals at the top with some small stitches. The skirt can either be tied on, or stitched on if you want it to remain permanently in place!

ADDING THE FINISHING TOUCHES

1. To make Betty's hair, needle the mohair locks into her head (see photo). Keep adding more ringlets until she has a fine head of hair.

2. Make a hairband from a few strands of the knitting yarn and sew on a few small flowers cut from leftover felt pieces. Place the completed garland on her curls.

3. Finally sew the feather wings to her back.

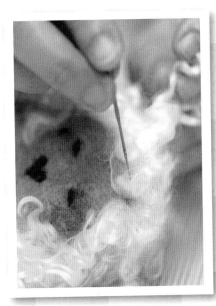

Ouch!

STRAWBERRY DEERSTALKER BABY HAT

Sweet and full of summer goodness all year round, this cute strawberry hat will keep your baby or toddler warm on the chilliest of days. It is made from two layers of wool around a plastic template, and, after the sides have been turned up and cut to shape, the stalk and leaves are made and added as a finishing touch.

TECHNIQUES
3-D SEAMLESS OBJECTS (PAGE 124),
SIMPLE FLAT FELT (PAGE 120),
MAKING A HANDLE/STRAND (PAGE 130)

MATERIALS

MERINO WOOL TOPS
2 oz (50 g) each of retro red and cherry red
1 oz (25 g) of racing green
⅔ oz (20 g) of dark olive
Small amount of gold

OTHER REQUIREMENTS
Wet felting essentials (see page 116)
Strong template plastic

Finished size: suitable for a one- to two-year old

NOTES
The template provided on page 139 is suitable for a one- to two-year old, so adjust accordingly for your baby or toddler.

Alternatively, to make a custom-fitted hat, take one of your little one's foldable hats, fold in half, trace around and increase by 20% overall, adding a further 10% in length for the ear flaps.

METHOD

WET FELTING THE HAT SHAPE

1. Cut your hat template from strong plastic (see notes, page 110). Lay out the first layer of cherry red vertically, overlapping the edges of the template. Cover with netting, wet, soap and rub for a few minutes. Turn the template over and fold in the edges. Repeat on the other side to complete the inner layer.

2. For the top layer, lay out the retro red in the opposite direction allowing for a generous overlap. Randomly add small wispy gold spots—for the strawberry "pips"—all over.

3. Cover, wet, soap and rub for about 20–30 minutes, or until all the fibers are securely attached together. Turn over and fold in the edges.

4. You are now working on the final side. Repeat step 2 to fill in the center section, remembering that no overlap is required this time. Cover, wet, soap and rub for a further 30 minutes. Make sure all the fibers are well felted together.

5. Briefly rinse in warm water, then do a complete roll on both sides as described on page 127 (see 3-d Seamless Objects, step 9). Rinse under very hot water, then roll briefly again, but take care not to shrink the hat too much!

6. Carefully cut open along the base of the hat, and remove the template.

FITTING AND SHAPING THE HAT

1. Now fold up a brim all the way around until the hat is the correct depth for the child's head. Cut the ear flaps at the side and a scalloped front edge (optional) using sharp scissors, inserting pins or a paper template for guidance, as you prefer.

2. Turn up the ear flaps and sew to the side of the hat using matching thread and tiny stitches.

MAKING THE STALK

1. Make a small square of flat felt using ⅔ oz (20 g) of dark olive for the first layer and ⅔ oz (20 g) of racing green for the second layer.

2. Using the template on page 139, cut a five-pointed strawberry leaf from the felt and sew through its center onto the top of the hat.

3. Use the full width of the remaining racing green wool to make a thick strand (see Making a Handle/Strand, page 130) and cut it to the appropriate length, using one uncut tapering end for the top of the stalk.

4. Mark the stalk's position in the middle of the leaf with a small blob of glue and sew in place with matching thread.

MAKING THE TIES

1. Use the remaining retro red and cherry red wool tops to make two felt strands just long enough to tie together safely under the your little one's chin.

2. Attach to the inside of the hat on either side with small stitches.

TECHNIQUES

EQUIPMENT AND MATERIALS

There isn't too much equipment required for felting, so it should be easy to find the things you need without too much trouble. The main requirement is your time— and plenty of elbow grease!

WORKSPACE

When wet felting, ideally you should work on a reasonably large table or workspace near to a sink. Hot and cold running water is a must. I encourage feltmaking using minimal amounts of water, so whilst flooding the room is unlikely, the odd soapy splash should be expected, and your work surface should be protected as necessary.

When needle felting, no water or soap is required, so just a small table space is all that is needed.

OTHER USEFUL EQUIPMENT

As well as the specific equipment required for the felting techniques, you may also need the items listed below. Other requirements will be given at the start of each project:

- Cutting mat
- Sharp craft knife
- Large sewing scissors
- Small, sharp embroidery scissors
- Pins
- Needle and thread
- Bodkin or large, sharp needle

WET FELTING ESSENTIALS

NETTING
You will need a piece of medium-weight polyester netting to lay over your fibers before wetting them. This will enable you to start rubbing the fibers with minimal disturbance of your design.

SOAPY WATER SOLUTION
Make a mixture of lukewarm water with a dash of dishwashing liquid. You will need some sort of receptacle to dispense it from slowly. I find it useful to have a clean plastic ketchup bottle when working with large, thick layers of fiber, and a spray bottle for smaller or more delicate projects, which require less water. You can also pierce small holes in the top of a clean drinks bottle, or use a sports cap bottle.

BAR OF SOAP
Any soap will do! The alkalinity of the soap is what's important here as it speeds up the feltmaking process, and its slipperiness aids rubbing.

DISH CLOTH AND JUG
To eliminate the risk of overwetting your fibers, you will use a dish cloth to mop up excess water and spread retained water through the wool fibers. Keep a jug, bowl or plastic container handy to squeeze the dish cloth out into.

BAMBOO MAT OR BLIND
Once the first stage of the felting process is complete and the fulling stage begins, using a bamboo mat is the best option for achieving fast, effective results, and that is what I use throughout this book. (Bubble wrap can be substituted if necessary, but it is less effective.) You will need a mat that is large enough to fit your project into; a bamboo blind is ideal, but a smaller bamboo mat is sometimes useful when you are making smaller items.

OLD TOWELS AND TEA TOWELS
These are great for mopping up excess water, and also for laying under the bamboo mat to keep it in place during the rolling process. It is imperative that you dry your hands in between rubbing wet felt and touching dry wool, so always keep a dry towel close by.

3-D FELTING ESSENTIALS

◆◆◆◆◆◆◆◆◆◆◆◆◆◆◆◆

STRONG TEMPLATE PLASTIC

For several of the projects in this book, including the Floribunda Folly Evening Bag (page 10) and A Felted Spectacle Glasses Case (page 19), you will need to cut a template from strong, thick plastic as a template to make the seamless 3-d shape from felt. This template plastic should be about 1000 microns thick, firm enough to retain its shape when hot, but flexible enough so you can feel the edge of it even through several layers of wool.

SHOE LASTS

Polystyrene shoe lasts (forms) are required for Contrary Mary's Garden Slippers (page 26) and Cozy-Go-Lightly Toddler Slippers (page 91). These generally come in US child's size 3–4 (European 18/19) for the smallest, to US men's size 11$\frac{1}{2}$–12$\frac{1}{2}$ (European 46/47) for the largest. The sizing is approximate so it's best to size up a little if you are unsure, as you can always shrink them a bit, but you can't make them bigger! If you wrap the shoe lasts in plastic bags when felting, you can re-use them.

NEEDLE FELTING ESSENTIALS

◆◆◆◆◆◆◆◆◆◆◆◆◆◆◆◆

PROTECTIVE FOAM

Use a rectangle of dense foam under all your needle felting. This will protect your table, and it will also protect YOU if you are not working at a table!

FELTING NEEDLES

You will need a selection of different sized felting needles for different types of work. The needles have small barbs at one end, which catch and entangle the fibers as you stab them in and out. The larger needles (36-gauge) are better suited to sculptural work, while smaller, finer needles (38-gauge) should be used for general and decorative work. They will last for a long time if used correctly and should not be used with force. Felting needles are extremely sharp, so use them with caution and take care.

MULTI-NEEDLE TOOL

This allows you to work with more than one needle at once and is ideal for larger areas.

WOOL TOPS

WHAT ARE WOOL TOPS?

A wool top is wool that has been taken from the sheep, cleaned (scoured) and combed (carded) so that all the fibers face the same way. It is wound into a continuous length and sold by weight. It is perfect for felting as the fibers are easily pulled from one end of the length. Wool roving is very similar to wool top, but the fibers do not necessarily all lie in the same direction, and it is for this reason that I always use wool tops for my feltmaking.

MERINO WOOL TOPS

Merino wool is the most commonly used for felting. Merino sheep like a warm climate and produce very fine wool with a fine crimp. This wool therefore felts the fastest and is often the one dyed into the many inspiring colors that we use for feltmaking. The Merino wool tops that I use are 64 count/23 micron (see the Wool Grading box).

EXPERIMENTING WITH OTHER WOOL TOPS

Any wool will felt—eventually—but, if you are interested in experimenting, it is worth bearing in mind that some wool will require a great deal more rubbing and working than others.

Different sheep breeds are all graded differently according to fiber length and thickness. Some British wools commonly used for felting are Blue Faced Leicester, Shetland, Moorit and Jacob—to name but a few. As you experiment with different wools, you will notice how some feel rougher and thicker and produce differing results. You should always remember that, if you are combining different breeds and grades of wool into the same project, it may take a lot longer to achieve the desired result as they will felt at different rates.

USING OTHER FIBERS AND PRE-FELT SHAPES

It is possible to add all sorts of other interesting fiber additions to the felt, as long as they are trapped in place with a little wool. For example, adding silk tops to the wool will result in more luster and a slightly different texture and outcome, as seen in the blue version of the Variegated Vintage Plant Baskets (page 80). Also see how the addition of some wool nepps (tiny textural wool balls) and Angelina fiber (glitter strands) to the Banqueting Bunting (page 36) adds to the decorative effect.

Pre-felt is simply "half made" felt that isn't too matted together and will still be accepted into new wool tops. Pre-felt shapes can be bought or made to add into the wool in more defined shapes, as has been done to make the daisy circle design that decorates the Carnival Carry All Bag (page 30).

CARE AND MAINTENANCE TIPS

◆◆◆◆◆◆◆◆◆◆◆◆◆◆◆◆◆

STORING WOOL TOPS

Always store wool away from moisture. Too much moisture—even from the air—makes wool start to felt and it will become matted, which makes it harder to work with. Storing the wool tops in plastic bags does no harm, and you should take care to repel moths. NEVER touch your wool with wet hands—wool is so much harder to work with once it has become wet, then dried again.

STORING PARTLY FINISHED PROJECTS

If you can't finish a wet felt project in one sitting, it's fine to leave it in an OPEN plastic bag and go back to it another day (do not seal the bag as the felt will go moldy and smell). You will more than likely have to re-wet the fibers if you leave the felt for more than an hour or so.

CLEANING FINISHED FELT

After your finished felt has been used for a while it may need cleaning—particularly lighter colors. I don't often wash pieces of felt as it can make the fabric shrink further. First try pulling off pilling and wipe down with a damp cloth. If washing is definitely necessary, hand wash only in lukewarm water with a mild wool detergent to prevent any further felting from taking place. Extremes of temperature and too much soap should be avoided. Never use a washing machine unless my project instructions specifically advise you to (or unless you are experimenting!).

SIMPLE FLAT FELT

◆◆◆◆◆◆◆◆◆◆◆◆◆◆◆◆◆◆◆◆◆◆◆◆◆◆◆

Simple flat felt is the easiest sort to make and a good place to start if you've never felted before. It will get you used to handling wool fibers and give you an understanding of the felting process before tackling more complex projects. Wool tops are separated and laid out into specific layers and patterns before being covered with netting and rubbed with soap and water. After the fibers have started to bond together, a series of rinsing and rolling in a bamboo mat further shrinks and hardens the felt (the "fulling" process). In addition, my technique for "precision" wet felting explains fine re-alignment of patterns and designs, and helps you to achieve successful outcomes where your designs end up exactly as intended!

STEP-BY-STEP WET FELTING TECHNIQUE

◆◆◆◆◆◆◆◆◆◆◆◆◆◆◆◆◆

BEFORE YOU START

- Decide on the size of the finished piece, remembering it will shrink by 15–20%.
- Get your wool and equipment ready, and protect your work surface, as it will get wet.
- Work on a bamboo mat, or directly onto a waterproof worktop, as you prefer.

1. PULLING OFF FIBERS

Hold the wool top length about 6 in. (15 cm) from the end with your left hand (if right-handed). Use your writing hand to pull the very ends of the fibers gently upward. The wool should come away easily and be fairly fine and wispy. If the wool is difficult to pull away, you may be grabbing too much at once, or your hands may be too close together, preventing the length of the wool fibers from becoming free. For a fine finished piece of felt, it is important to pull off fine even amounts of wool rather than clumps, so do practice to get the technique right.

2. LAYING OUT FIBERS

Lay the wool overlapping slightly, building it up gradually to create a fine, even layer. Use sufficient wool so you can no longer see through it to the surface beneath—it should appear to be a solid color. At this stage the layer is mostly air and once the wool has been wet down it will be much flatter.

3. LAYING SUBSEQUENT LAYERS

Most flat felt is made up of two or three layers. Each layer is laid in the opposite direction to the previous one, to achieve more even shrinkage and to make the finished felt more robust. You can use more layers for a piece that needs to be thicker and hardwearing.

4. BUILDING A DESIGN

To add your design on the top of the background layers, use very small amounts of wool tops. Tease the wool apart to make it fine and sheer (larger clumps of wool will not attach together as the fibers will be too tightly coiled and won't be able to tangle together sufficiently). Place these small pieces of wool tops out into your design, manipulating and teasing the fibers to lie as desired. You can add further wool on top in a similar manner to achieve more solid colors, but build up the designs gradually. Take particular care when creating spots and dots as these will refuse to bond together if they are too tightly coiled.

5. ADDING TEXTURAL HIGHLIGHTS

It is possible to trap glitter strands, silk, nepps and other interesting fibers into your felt for interest and texture, but use sparingly. Always place a small cobwebby amount of wool over the top of added fibers; this will ensure that they felt to the background layer.

6. WETTING DOWN

Carefully lay the netting over the fibers. Use a squeezy bottle to sprinkle soapy water over the netting. Hold the netting in place with one hand and use your other hand to spread the soapy water through using a dish cloth. It is important that every fiber is completely wet and soapy, and that all the air is removed. It should feel as if the wool is stuck to the table with soapy glue: if it still feels springy to the touch, more soapy water is required; if it feels puddly and over wet, mop up a little. There is a fine line between too little and too much liquid—the fibers need to be wet through thoroughly, but if they are swimming in water it will prevent the felting from taking place as quickly.

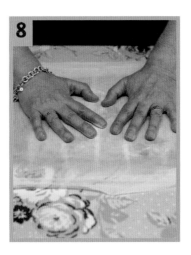

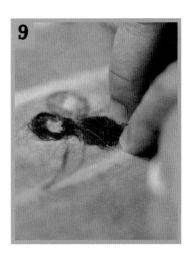

7. SOAPING UP

Rub a bar of soap over the netting to make it slippery (there should be enough soapy suds to draw a picture in). This is a vital part of the felting process. The soap encourages the felting to take place by getting the microscopic scales on the wool fibers to start to swell, move open and eventually lock together.

8. RUBBING

Keeping the netting flat and taut, rub with both hands and plenty of pressure to encourage the fibers to entangle. Some fibers may cling to the net as you rub. Peel back the net, remove the fibers and replace the net in a slightly different position to prevent permanent adherence. Keep rubbing for 10 minutes or so.

9. PRECISION WET FELTING

Adding the soapy water can move and distort your created design, so to make sure your felt ends up as you intended, it is important to make adjustments during the rubbing process. Start by peeling back the netting almost immediately after soaping up and re-adjust the fibers that may have moved, using your fingers or the ends of some small scissors. Replace the netting and rub for a little longer and then repeat the adjustments. Keep doing this now and again during the first 10 minutes of rubbing before the fibers start to take hold.

10. TESTING FELTING

To test if the felt is sufficiently rubbed, remove the netting and briskly rub your hand across it. If the fibers no longer move around, you are done. If any areas wobble, replace the net and continue to rub until everything is well held together.

11. RINSING

Rinse gently using lukewarm water. Do not immerse or leave under the tap for too long as the felt is still very delicate; simply show it the water, then wring gently. Repeat several times until most of the soap is removed. Squeeze out excess water.

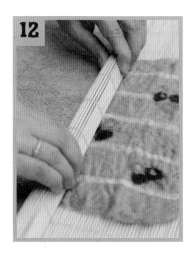

12. ROLLING UP YOUR FELT

To further shrink and harden your work and turn it into a robust and finished piece of felt, it is now rolled in a bamboo mat, which provides good friction as it pushes backward and forward against the slats. There are other ways of doing this, but the bamboo mat method is the fastest and most effective in my opinion. It is vital to roll up the felt as tightly as possible as this makes it much easier to roll. Place an old towel under the mat to prevent it from sliding about.

13. ROLLING THE FELT IN ALL DIRECTIONS

The felt will start to shrink in the direction you laid the fibers out in and the direction it is rolled in, so to achieve an even shrinkage it is necessary to keep rotating the felt as you roll. Roll the mat back and forth with a firm, even pressure about 20 times. Unroll, turn the felt 90° clockwise and then repeat. Continue through 360°, then turn the felt over and repeat on the other side.

14. FINAL RINSING AND FINISHING

The felt is now far more robust and you can really manipulate it during the final rinse to ensure that all the soap is removed. (It is vital to remove all traces of soap to prevent the felt from rotting in the future.) Use lukewarm water if you want to prevent too much further shrinkage during the rinsing process. Extremes of temperature will cause much greater shrinkage, and if this is not a concern, you can rinse with very hot water and then very cold. Once soap free, remove as much water as possible and roll again briefly to flatten. To shrink further, repeat the entire rolling process again. Lay flat to dry naturally in a warm place; finish with a warm iron if desired.

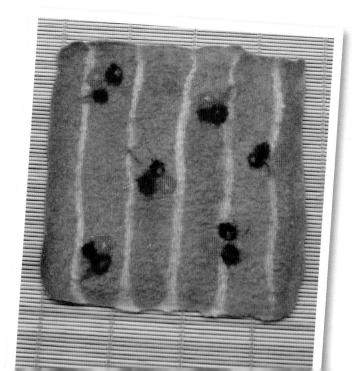

The finished piece.

◆◆◆◆◆◆◆◆◆◆◆◆◆◆◆◆◆◆◆◆

3-D SEAMLESS OBJECTS

◆◆◆◆◆◆◆◆◆◆◆◆◆◆◆◆◆◆◆◆◆◆◆◆◆

By layering wool around specially cut plastic templates and 3-d forms such as shoe lasts, you can create strong seamless objects without any sewing. Wool is layered over the template or last one side at a time, with an overlap around the edges. The overlap is then turned in on the other side and the new layer is laid over the top. As the layers are built up—working from the inner layer through to the outer layer—the template or last becomes totally encased in wool. Finally, the felted shape is cut open with a pair of sharp scissors and the template or last removed, to leave the felt that was created around it.

STEP-BY-STEP HOLLOW FORM TECHNIQUE

◆◆◆◆◆◆◆◆◆◆◆◆◆◆◆◆◆

BEFORE YOU START

- Get your materials ready, and protect your work surface as it will get wet.
- Cut your template to shape from strong, flexible plastic (see page 117) remembering that the finished piece will shrink by 15–20%.
- Decide how many layers thick you want your object to be. Generally speaking I tend to make most medium-sized bags three layers thick, so that they are strong enough to hold what is put inside them without stretching and distorting. Use four or more layers to make even larger items, so they will be more robust when finished.

For a tea cozy, or for smaller objects that don't get a lot of use, two layers will be fine. Note, the instructions that follow are for three layers.

1. PULLING AND LAYING FIBERS FOR THE INNER LAYER

Lay down the wool for the INSIDE of your project first. Referring to Simple Flat Felt, steps 1 and 2, lay the wool across the template with all the fibers facing in the same direction. Overlap the edges of the template all the way around by about 1 in. (2–3 cm).

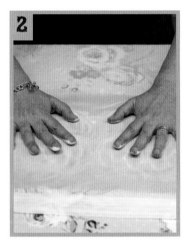

2. WETTING, SOAPING AND RUBBING

Referring to Simple Flat Felt, steps 6 and 7, cover the fibers with the netting, wet them down, and make them flat and soapy. Begin to rub (see Simple Flat Felt, step 8) but only for about five minutes to start the fibers felting a little bit (if they felt together too much, they won't then accept the new fibers you will be adding for the subsequent layers).

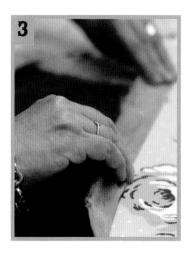

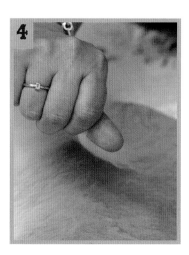

3. COMPLETING THE INNER LAYER

Remove the netting and boldly turn the whole thing over. Fold in the overlapped side seams, keeping them tight into the edges of the template. Repeat steps 1 and 2 on this side of the template, still overlapping all the way around.

4. LAYING THE MIDDLE LAYER

Remove the netting, turn the whole thing over again and fold in the overlapped edges as before. Now add the first side of the middle layer, which is trapped or sandwiched between the inner and outer layers. (The middle layer is seen when the felt shape is cut open, and some fibers may travel through from one side to another, so carefully choose a co-ordinating color to match the inner and outer layers.) This time lay the fibers facing in the opposite direction, adding overlap as before, then cover, wet, soap and rub as in step 2. Repeat on the other side to complete the middle layer.

5. LAYING THE FIRST SIDE OF THE OUTER LAYER

Remove the netting, turn over again and fold in the seams. Lay the background color(s) for the outer layer in the opposite direction to the middle layer (i.e. in the same direction as the first inner layer), providing for a larger than normal overlap around the edge on this side to allow for finishing off on the next—and final—side. Referring to Simple Flat Felt, step 4, add your designs on top of the background color(s), making sure to use the wool finely and wispily.

6. COVERING AND RUBBING THE PENULTIMATE SIDE

Cover with the netting, wet, soap and rub for 20–30 minutes, depending on the size of the project you are making. Peel back the netting as many times as necessary and re-adjust your design to keep it as you'd intended (see Simple Flat Felt, step 9, page 122). Make sure there is plenty of soap, but check that there is not too much water in the wool at this point, as this may prevent the fibers from felting together. It should feel sudsy without being puddle-like. If necessary reduce excess liquid by running a dry cloth over the netting. Rub until the fibers feel fixed and no longer move around when brushed against briskly.

7. LAYING AND RUBBING THE FINAL SIDE

Turn the whole thing over once more; fold in the generous overlap. Lay out the background wool, but do not allow for an overlap this time. Keep the fibers at least ³⁄₈ in. (1 cm) from the edge to prevent an overhang when you wet the wool down, and make them fine and cobwebby as you lay them out so no hard lines form. Lay down your design on top, cover with the netting, wet, soap, and rub for 20–30 minutes. Once the fibers feel well fixed together, remove the netting and rub all over with wet soapy hands, particularly around the edges. It should all feel solid, together, rougher and slightly bobbly. If you are confident that the design is firmly attached, move on to rinse; if not, rub some more.

8. RINSING

Rinse the felt briefly in lukewarm water. Just show it the water and then wring several times in succession. Whatever you do, do not leave the felt under a running tap or immerse it in the sink, as it is still quite delicate at this stage. Try to get most of the soap out now before you move on (if there is still a lot of soap remaining, your item will shrink much more quickly). Wring out well but gently.

9. ROLLING

To further shrink and harden your work and turn it into a robust and finished piece of felt, it is now rolled in a bamboo mat. Lay a towel under the mat to prevent slipping; roll up your felt into the mat as tightly as possible, as this makes it easier to roll. Roll back and forth with a firm, even pressure about 20 times. To achieve an even shrinkage it is necessary to keep rotating the felt. Unroll, turn the felt 90° clockwise and then repeat. Continue through 360°, turning 90° each time, then turn the felt over and repeat on the other side.

10. CUTTING OPEN

Rinse in hot water and repeat the rolling as in step 9 but this time allowing for only 10 times per roll. Using small sharp scissors, start to cut open the top edge for a bag or the bottom edge for a tea cozy. Once you have found the template inside, push it out of the way and continue across with larger scissors, then remove the template. Trim the edges straight if necessary—or cut a scalloped edge if desired—then rub the newly cut edges with more soapy water and soap for about 5–10 minutes to felt them.

11. FINAL RINSING

It is vital to remove all traces of soap, so go back to the sink and rinse again using hot water first, then freezing cold (or to prevent further shrinkage, lukewarm water). Keep rinsing and wringing until all the soap is removed. Give your finished article a final roll to flatten before leaving to dry in a warm place. (Note, if you want to achieve further shrinkage, further rinsing and rolling can be undertaken.)

The finished piece.

❖ ❖ ❖ ❖ ❖ ❖ ❖ ❖ ❖ ❖ ❖ ❖ ❖ ❖

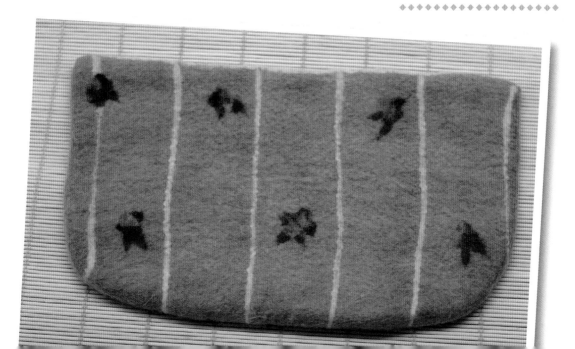

USING A SHOE LAST

BEFORE YOU START

- First select the size of polystyrene shoe lasts (form) you require, following the advice on page 117.

1. PREPARING THE LASTS

Cover each shoe last with a plastic bag and secure the bag with an elastic band at the top, trimming off the excess. Mist down with some soapy water to help the first layer stick to the plastic and prevent it from sliding straight off. Work each layer on one foot at a time.

2. LAYING FIBERS

Starting with the sole, lay half the fibers down from the toe to the heel (the wool should overlap the ends slightly), then lay the other half over the top in the opposite direction. Use a small bamboo mat —or similar—to help prop up each shoe last as you work on it.

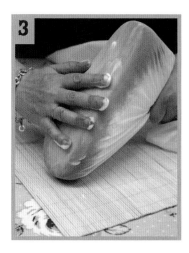 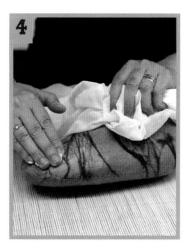 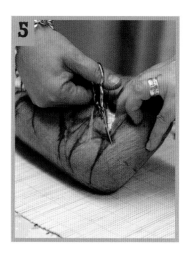

3. COVER, SOAP AND RUB

Cover with netting and pull the edges of the netting together so you can hold with one hand, leaving your other hand free to mist down the wool through the net, using the soapy water. Use a dish cloth to spread the soapy water through the fibers, making sure they are flat and thoroughly wet through (and no longer springy). Add plenty of soap and rub for about five minutes, but no longer.

4. ADDING FURTHER LAYERS

Repeat the laying, wetting, soaping and rubbing process on one side of the last, and then on the other side, each time overlapping the edges slightly to make sure that the last is completely covered, including the very top. Add further layers in the same way. On the outer and final layer, add a design BEFORE rubbing, and then rub each final layer for about 30 minutes, or until the fibers no longer move when you brush your hand across them.

5. REMOVING FELT FROM THE LASTS

After washing the slippers on a 140°F (60°C) wash cycle in your washing machine (add an old pair of jeans or similar to facilitate the felting process), it is time to remove the felt from the lasts, using small sharp scissors to cut them away. This can be done wet, or dry.

Decide first on the slipper shape you would like. For a mule (as shown), use pins to create the lines of each slipper before you cut the back away and ease out the lasts. Always leave a small cup at the back of the heel. For an adult bootie, it is necessary to make a small cut around the very top and also down the front about 2 in. (5 cm) long in order to remove the last. Trim the top edges neatly and leave to dry.

HANDLES AND STRANDS, BEADS AND BALLS

◆◆◆◆◆◆◆◆◆◆◆◆◆◆◆◆◆◆◆◆◆◆

You can make all sorts of useful felt shapes by manipulating and compacting wool tops—from handles for bags, to felted strands, beads and balls. This can add decorative interest to your finished projects. Handles and strands are made in exactly the same way using differing widths of wool tops. The more wool used widthways, the thicker they will be. Beads can be cut from a felt sausage made in the same way as a handle, but including lots of different colors in the middle. A ball is simply rolled up wool that is felted together with soap and water.

MAKING A HANDLE/STRAND
◆◆◆◆◆◆◆◆◆◆◆◆◆◆◆◆◆

BEFORE YOU START

- Get your wool and equipment ready, and protect your work surface as it will get wet. You will need a bamboo mat, but no netting is required.
- You will need a sharp craft knife and cutting mat to cut up the beads from a felt sausage or slice balls in half.
- For handles and strands, and bead sausages, twist the wool tops tightly to remove air to work out how wide they will be once felted. Always remember the wool will shrink in length too, by about 15–20%.
- Balls can shrink quite dramatically during the felting process (as much as 50%), so allow for this when selecting your wool.

1. CHOOSING WOOLS

For a handle, use the full width of the wool. To make a fine strand that could potentially fit through the eye of a large needle or bodkin (as in the Crowning Glory Chandelier, page 59), pull away a very fine length of wool to suit.

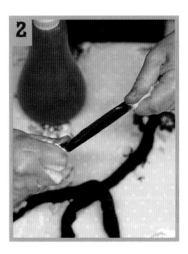

2. WETTING AND SOAPING

Wet the handle (or strand, working on only one at a time) with soapy water from a spray bottle until thoroughly wet through to the core; wring out slightly so it is not dripping wet. Make your hands very soapy and keep pulling the wool length gently through your hand for about five minutes until you notice it begin to harden slightly—do not pull too hard or it will pull apart.

3. ROLLING

Make sure the wool is adequately wet (but not sopping) and very soapy. Place on the bamboo mat and flip the end of the mat over the top. Start to roll back and forth with plenty of pressure, up and down the length of the wool. If the piece is longer than the width of your mat, you will need to feed it through, taking care to work on all parts of the length. As it hardens, you can snake it around into the mat and roll together. It is important to keep the soap levels up, adding more now and again as you roll. Halfway through, you can pour boiling water over the top to aid shrinkage and hardening. Do this in the sink and take care not to scald yourself; leave to cool before you carry on rolling.

4. RINSING AND FINISHING

The rolling time required will differ depending on the thickness of the wool you've used; a handle width will probably take about 20–30 minutes, but a fine strand could be felted in just 10 minutes. Once you are confident that you have achieved sufficient felted rigidity, rinse out all the soap. Working on a soap-free bamboo mat, roll out again to finish.

TIP

For thinner strands you may find it more comfortable to roll the sausage directly onto the bamboo.

MAKING A BEAD SAUSAGE

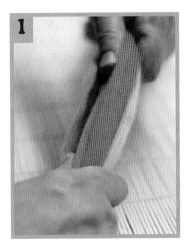

1. CHOOSING WOOLS

Bunch together lots of pieces of wool to the desired thickness. Gather together as many different lengths and colors as you need—odds and ends are ideal for this —and twist them together tightly to get some indication of the finished width. You can change the colors you use up and down the length of the sausage, so that when it is cut up, all your beads will be different.

2. WRAPPING WITH AN OUTER LAYER

Lay out a finer continuous piece of wool as an outer jacket and roll the other pieces up in it. Make this as thick or as thin as you like, to achieve different effects. It is important that this wool is well held together around the outside, without too many channels and folds. Be warned—the more wool you incorporate and the thicker the sausage, the longer it takes to felt together!

3. FELTING THE SAUSAGE

Wet, soap, roll and rinse following Making a Handle/Strand, steps 2, 3 and 4, pages 130–131. The rolling time will depend on the thickness of the wool you've used, but is likely to take at least an hour, if not longer. It is particularly important that the bead sausage is rock hard all the way through to the center core, otherwise the beads will appear fluffy when cut up. Rinsing time is also likely to take longer.

4. CUTTING BEADS

Working on a cutting mat, take a sharp craft knife and carve off one bead at a time. Make each bead a significant width so it will be strong enough to thread on.

MAKING A BALL

◆◆◆◆◆◆◆◆◆◆◆◆◆◆◆◆◆

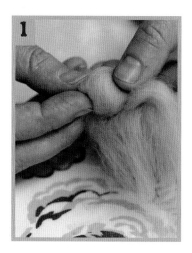

1. COILING UP WOOL

Gather together some wool tops and roll them up into a tight ball. Wrap further wool around this core to create different color combinations or patterns, and wrap a final wispy piece of wool top around the outside to keep everything in place. This will prevent channels forming, and will ensure that the ball does not end up looking like a shrivelled brain! Remember the finished ball can shrink by about 15–40% depending on how tightly you coil the wool, so coil up the ball larger than you want it to end up. Do a test one if necessary, and if you need several the same size, then coil the dry wool up first for all of them, and felt them one by one.

2. WETTING, ROLLING AND RINSING

Holding the felt ball tightly, wet it down with some of the soapy water solution until wet through to the core. Wring out excess water and make it—and your hands—very soapy. Start to roll the ball very lightly in between your palms, using as little pressure as possible to avoid squashing it before it has begun to harden. After 5–10 minutes, you should notice the ball starting to feel much harder and denser; now move on to rolling it on the bamboo mat and begin to apply more pressure as it hardens. When firm, rinse thoroughly in hot water until all traces of soap are removed.

3. CUTTING AND NEEDLE FELTING

Balls cut in half make excellent flower centers for daisies. Always use a sharp craft knife and work on a cutting mat. You could also add decorative needle felt designs onto the balls by simply stabbing in some wool with a felting needle (see Needle Felting, page 134).

NEEDLE FELTING

◆◆◆◆◆◆◆◆◆◆◆◆◆◆◆◆◆◆◆◆◆◆◆◆◆◆◆◆

Needle felting is a dry felting technique that uses very sharp, barbed needles to push fibers up and down until they start to tangle and bond together. Although the process is very different from wet felting, the end result is the same—felted wool that has matted together and shrunk. It lends itself to applying fine details and precise decorative accents. It is great for joining felt together and ideal for sculpting and making solid shapes, so it works well in combination with wet felting. It is often referred to as embellishing. While embellishing machines are available, working with one or more needles by hand is just as successful and much cheaper.

DECORATIVE NEEDLE FELTING

◆◆◆◆◆◆◆◆◆◆◆◆◆◆◆◆◆◆

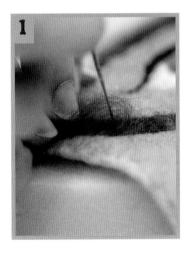  

1. ATTACHING MOTIFS

Decorations and fine details can be added onto a felt background using very small amounts of wispy wool placed in the appropriate position (this is ideal for using small leftover scraps). Keep the felting needle perpendicular to your work and stab gently to avoid needle breakage. As the wool disappears into the felt, add more if necessary, and build up designs gradually using other colors. (To attach larger motifs you can use a multi-needle tool if you desire.) Every now and again lift your work off the protective foam to avoid attachment.

2. CORRECTING MISTAKES

If you don't like what you've done, it's easy to carefully pick off the wool with the end of the needle and start again, provided it is not too firmly embedded.

TIP
When needle felting onto a flat piece of felt or fabric, place protective foam underneath it to protect the work surface.

◆◆◆◆◆◆◆◆◆◆◆◆◆◆◆◆◆◆◆

3. RAISED NEEDLE FELTING

By using slightly more wool and needling slightly less onto it, it is possible to create decorative raised areas of needle felting to add depth and textural interest, as has been achieved on the Candy-Coated Cupcake Tea Cozy, page 76. Bunch up small pieces of wool top and needle on together to form raised bumps. Add further cobwebby wool in between, and experiment by needling just around the edges of each bump rather than all over.

SCULPTURAL NEEDLE FELTING

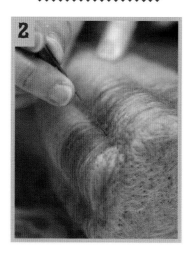

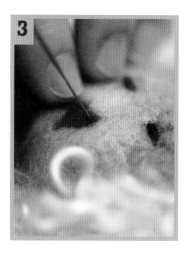

1. ROUGH SHAPING

Needle felted wool will shrink as the wool fibers become entangled and the air is removed. It is difficult to say how much by, and it will largely depend on how densely the wool is compacted together when you first start. Bunch together sufficient wool tops in the rough shape you need, and start to stab together. It is often easier and quicker at this stage to use a multi-needle tool with four large 36-gauge needles—depending on the size of the piece. Add on more wool as required and refine the shape as much as possible. This takes time and patience!

2. REFINING THE SHAPE

When the overall shape has been achieved, you can refine it using just one needle. Repeated stabbing with just one needle will create an indentation, which is useful for detailing smaller pieces.

WARNING
Felting needles are extremely sharp and not suitable for children to use. Take care not to stab yourself.

3. ADDING DETAILS

Add patterns and motifs in exactly the same way as Decorative Needle Felting opposite (see step 1, Attaching Motifs). The only difference is that no protective foam is required when attaching designs onto a sculpted base like this.

TEMPLATES

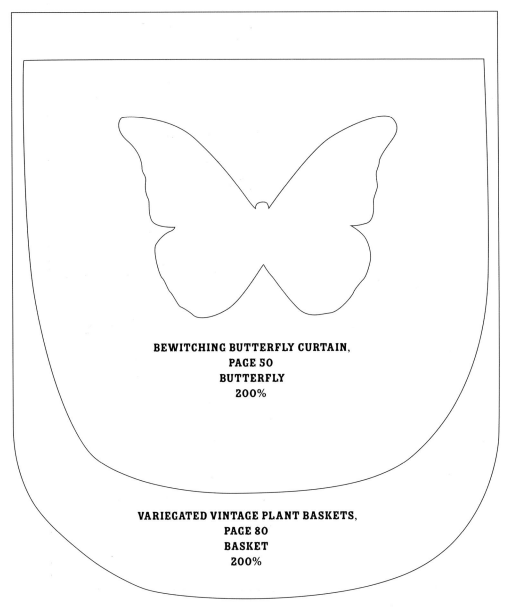

BEWITCHING BUTTERFLY CURTAIN,
PAGE 50
BUTTERFLY
200%

VARIEGATED VINTAGE PLANT BASKETS,
PAGE 80
BASKET
200%

FLORIBUNDA FOLLY EVENING BAG,
PAGE 12
BAG
200%

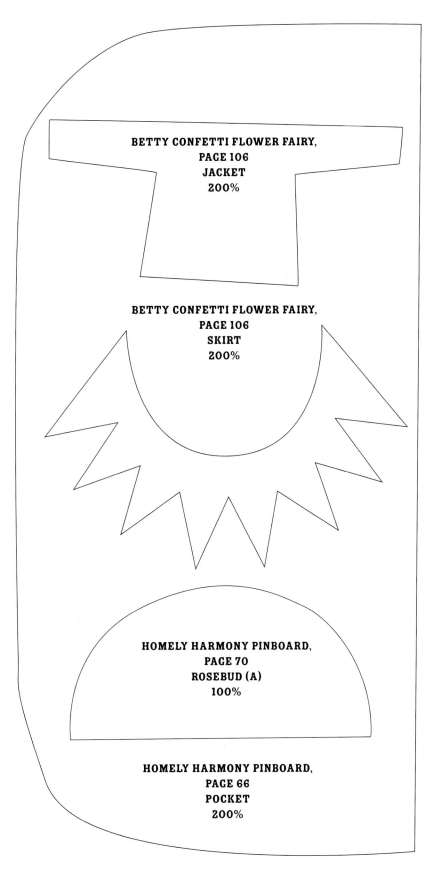

BETTY CONFETTI FLOWER FAIRY,
PAGE 106
JACKET
200%

BETTY CONFETTI FLOWER FAIRY,
PAGE 106
SKIRT
200%

HOMELY HARMONY PINBOARD,
PAGE 70
ROSEBUD (A)
100%

HOMELY HARMONY PINBOARD,
PAGE 66
POCKET
200%

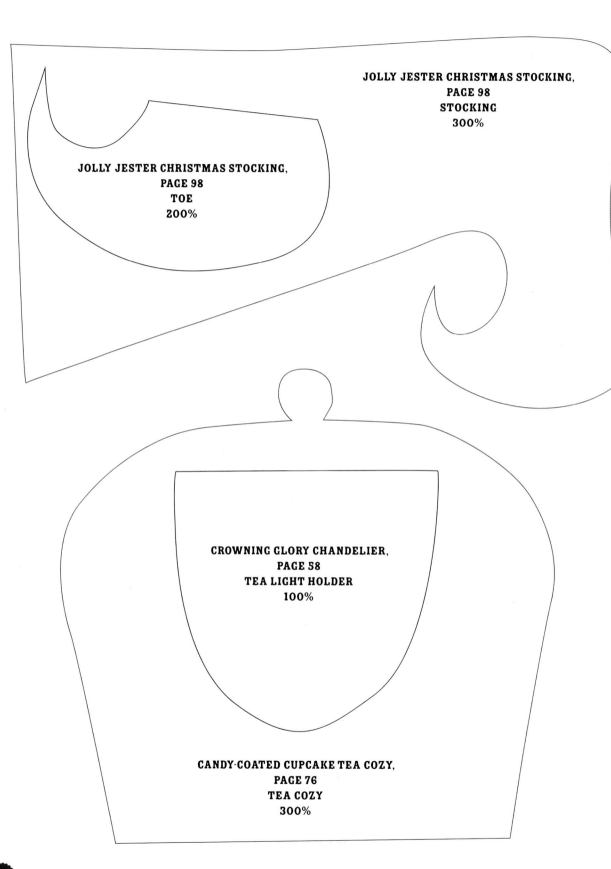

JOLLY JESTER CHRISTMAS STOCKING,
PAGE 98
STOCKING
300%

JOLLY JESTER CHRISTMAS STOCKING,
PAGE 98
TOE
200%

CROWNING GLORY CHANDELIER,
PAGE 58
TEA LIGHT HOLDER
100%

CANDY-COATED CUPCAKE TEA COZY,
PAGE 76
TEA COZY
300%

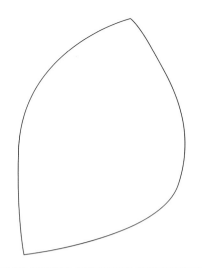

JOLLY JESTER CHRISTMAS STOCKING,
PAGE 98
HEEL
200%

STRAWBERRY DEERSTALKER BABY HAT,
PAGE 110
LEAF
200%

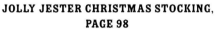

HOMELY HARMONY PINBOARD,
PAGE 70
ROSEBUD (B)
100%

EGGY PEGGY CLOTHESPIN BAG,
PAGE 84
BAG
300%

STRAWBERRY DEERSTALKER BABY HAT,
PAGE 110
HAT
200%

GLOSSARY

◆◆◆◆◆◆◆◆◆◆◆◆◆◆◆◆

ANGELINA® FIBER: A very fine, glittery and light reflective fiber that is sometimes heat bondable. Comes in three types: iridescent, holographic and metallized.

BATT: A carded mass of fleece that can be separated into layers. Used as an alternative to wool tops. Unlike wool tops, the fibers do not all face in the same direction. Often used in large expanses with felting needles to form flat sheets of needle felt.

BLOCK: A block is a form used in making and drying a piece to a desired shape. Hat blocks are often used when making felt hats.

BLOOD COUNT: An American method of grading wool, based on the percentage of Merino breed in the original sheep.

BOILED WOOL: Traditionally this is knitted wool that has been boiled in order to obscure the knitted stitches. Done in a controlled environment to produce an even cloth from very fine wool. Many wools will distort and lose their color at such a high temperature.

BRADFORD COUNT: A British wool grading system, which refers to the number of 560-yard skeins of wool from a pound weight. The higher the count, the finer the wool.

CARDING: A process very similar to hair brushing. Using either metal-pronged hand carders or a drum carder, the wool fibers are combed out into long, even lengths, so that all the fibers are facing in the same direction.

CRIMP: The waviness of the wool fibers. Finer wools have much more crimp per inch than coarser wools.

FELTING: The matting together of wool fibers to form a dense fabric that is stable and does not fray.

FELTING NEEDLES: The barbed needle that is repeatedly poked in and out of wool tops to produce flat or sculptural pieces of felt without the need for water. The barbs on the needle entangle the wool fibers as they are pulled in and out. Different gauge needles have different effects on the wool.

FLEECE: The wool from a sheep in one piece, containing lanolin. Also a term sometimes used to refer to wool tops being used for feltmaking.

FULLING: The final stage of shrinking and hardening the felt or knitted fabric to make it thicker and denser.

GAUGE: Refers to the size of a felting needle. The higher the gauge, the more delicate the needle. Fine needles are suited to a finer decorative application of fleece. The lower gauge needles are used for forming basic shapes and sculpting. The needles also come in different shapes; triangular and the multi-faceted star shape, which is faster to work with. Finer needles break more easily. In knitting, it refers to the number of knitted stitches and rows in a defined square.

HANDLE: The feel of a fiber or fabric.

LANOLIN: The grease or wax produced by the sebaceous glands of the sheep. It has waterproofing qualities, and prevents the sheep from becoming too wet. Although most is removed during scouring, what little remains has the added benefit of preventing sore, chapped hands after many hours of feltmaking. Lanolin is used by the pharmaceutical industry.

LASTS: Forms over which shoes or boots are made.

MICRON: A micron is a millionth of a meter (or 1/25,000 of an inch) and is the most accurate way of grading wool. The lower the micron, the finer the wool.

NUNO FELT: Felt that incorporates a fine fabric. It is most suitable for felt clothing, as the results maintain their draping qualities. Comes from the Japanese word "nuno" meaning fabric.

PRE-FELT: Half-made felt that is then inlaid into further projects on top of new wool tops, to create uniform designs that don't move around too much.

ROVING: Similar to tops, but the fibers do not always face the same direction.

SCALES: The tiny overlapping scales on the surface of the wool fibers, which open up from the base to the top and then lock together once they have entangled during felting. Hot water encourages the scales to open up and cold water to close again.

SCOURING: The act of washing the wool when it is first shorn to remove dirt, grease and bits of vegetation!

STAPLE LENGTH: The fiber length of wool, which varies according to the sheep.

TOPS: Wool tops refers to the continuous length of wool fibers produced during the carding process, in which all the fibers lie in the same direction—making them ideal for layering in felting. They are sold in different lengths, and are usually between 2–3 in. (2.5–7.5 cm) wide.

RESGURCES

◆◆◆◆◆◆◆◆◆◆◆◆◆◆◆◆

For Wool Tops, Wool Blends, Other Fibers including Angelina Fiber and Wash and Filz It Wool, Pre-felt Shapes, Trimmings, Felting Equipment and Needles, Handbag Handles, Slipper Lasts and Regia Slipper Soles, Felting Kits and Felting Courses:

The Gilliangladrag Fluff-a-torium
20 West Street, Dorking, Surrey
RH4 1BL UK
Tel: 01306 898144

www.gilliangladrag.co.uk
Worldwide shipping available

FOR TRIMMINGS AND RIBBONS:

Jo Ann Fabric and Crafts
www.joann.com

M&J Trimming
1008 Sixth Avenue
New York, NY 10018
Tel: (212) 204-9595
www.mjtrim.com

Michaels Arts and Crafts
www.michaels.com

FELTMAKING SUPPLIES:

Crown Mountain Farms
PO Box 2864
Velm, WA 98597
Tel: (866) 652-1738
www.crownmountainfarms.com

Marr Haven Wool Farm
772 39th Street
Allegan, MI 49010
Tel: (269) 673-8800
www.marrhaven.com

Outback Fibers
PO Box 55
Coaldale, CO 81222
Tel: (512) 222-WOOL
www.outbackfibers.com

Paradise Fibers
225 W. Indiana
Spokane, IN 99205
www.paradisefibers.com

The Woolery
315 St. Clair
Frankfort, KY 40601
Tel: (800) 441-9665
www.woolery.com

FOR FURTHER READING AND INFORMATION ON FELTMAKING:

International Feltmakers Association

www.feltmakers.com

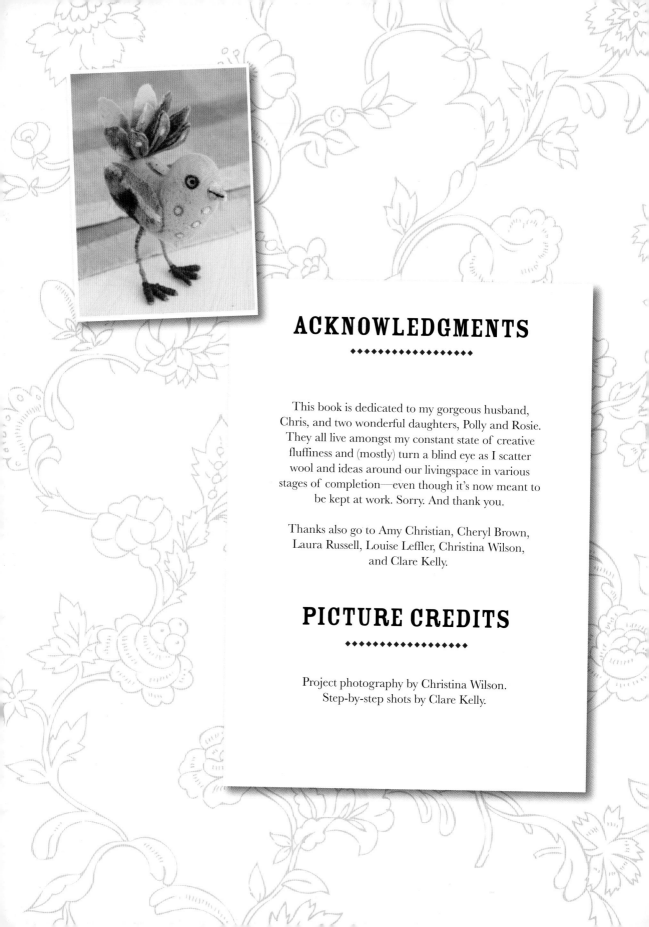

ACKNOWLEDGMENTS

◆◆◆◆◆◆◆◆◆◆◆◆◆◆◆◆◆◆

This book is dedicated to my gorgeous husband, Chris, and two wonderful daughters, Polly and Rosie. They all live amongst my constant state of creative fluffiness and (mostly) turn a blind eye as I scatter wool and ideas around our livingspace in various stages of completion—even though it's now meant to be kept at work. Sorry. And thank you.

Thanks also go to Amy Christian, Cheryl Brown, Laura Russell, Louise Leffler, Christina Wilson, and Clare Kelly.

PICTURE CREDITS

◆◆◆◆◆◆◆◆◆◆◆◆◆◆◆◆◆◆

Project photography by Christina Wilson.
Step-by-step shots by Clare Kelly.